THE MEANING

OF

Prayer

THE
MEANING
OF
Prayer

HARRY EMERSON FOSDICK

 941

ABINGDON PRESS
NASHVILLE

THE MEANING OF PRAYER

ISBN 0-687-23962-1
Previously published by Follett under ISBN 0-695-81088-X
and by Abingdon Press under ISBN 0-687-23960-5

Special acknowledgment is gladly made to the following: to the Pilgrim Press for permission to use selections from Dr. Rauschenbusch's *Prayers of the Social Awakening;* to E. P. Dutton & Company for permission to use prayers from *A Chain of Prayers Across the Ages;* to the Rev. Samuel McComb and the publishers for permission to draw upon *A Book of Prayer,* Copyright, 1912, Dodd, Mead & Company; to George W. Jacobs & Company for permission to make quotations from *The Communion of Prayer;* to Mrs. Mary W. Tileston for the use of *Prayers Ancient and Modern;* to Fleming H. Revell for permission to quote from Henry Ward Beecher's *Book of Public Prayer;* and to the author and publishers of W. E. Orchard's *The Temple,* E. P. Dutton & Company.

MANUFACTURED BY THE PARTHENON PRESS AT
NASHVILLE, TENNESSEE, UNITED STATES OF AMERICA

CONTENTS

CHAPTER I

The Naturalness of Prayer

DAILY READINGS

First Day, First Week

Samuel Johnson once was asked what the strongest argument for prayer was, and he replied, "Sir, there is no argument for prayer." One need only read Johnson's own petitions, such as the one below, to see that he did not mean by this to declare prayer irrational; he meant to stress the fact that praying is first of all a native tendency. It is a practice like breathing or eating in this respect, that men engage in it because they are human, and *afterward* argue about it as best they can. As Carlyle stated it in a letter to a friend: "Prayer is and remains the native and deepest impulse of the soul of man." Consider this universal tendency to pray as revealed in "Solomon's prayer" at the dedication of the temple:

Moreover concerning the foreigner, that is not of thy people Israel, when he shall come from a far country for thy great name's sake, and thy mighty hand, and thine outstretched arm; when they shall come and pray toward this house; then hear thou from heaven, even from thy dwelling place, and do according to all that the foreigner calleth to thee for; that all the peoples of the earth may know thy name, and fear thee, as doth thy people Israel, and that they may know that this house which I have built is called by thy name.—II Chron. 6:32, 33.

Note how this prayer takes for granted that any stranger coming from anywhere on earth is likely to be a praying man. Let us say to ourselves on this first day of our study, that in dealing with prayer we are dealing, as this Scripture suggests, with a natural function of human life.

> "All souls that struggle and aspire,
> All hearts of prayer, by thee are lit;
> And, dim or clear, thy tongues of fire
> On dusky tribes and twilight centuries sit."

O Lord, in whose hands are life and death, by whose power I am sustained, and by whose mercy I am spared, look down upon me with pity. Forgive me that I have until now so much neglected the duty which Thou hast assigned to me, and suffered the days and hours of which I must give account to pass away without any endeavor to accomplish Thy will. Make me to remember, O God, that every day is Thy gift, and ought to be used according to Thy command. Grant me, therefore, so to repent of my negligence, that I may obtain mercy from Thee, and pass the time which Thou shalt yet allow me in diligent performance of Thy commands, through Jesus Christ. Amen.—Samuel Johnson (1709-1784).

Second Day, First Week

Epictetus was a non-Christian philosopher and yet listen to him: "When thou hast shut thy door and darkened thy room, say not to thyself that thou art alone. God is in thy room." Read now Paul's appreciation of this hunger for God and this sense of his presence which are to be found among all peoples.

Ye men of Athens, in all things I perceive that ye are very religious. For as I passed along, and observed the objects of your worship, I found also an altar with this inscription, "To an Unknown God." What therefore ye worship in ignorance, this I set forth unto you. The God that made the world and all things therein, he, being Lord of heaven and earth, dwelleth not in temples made with hands; neither is he served by men's hands, as though he needed anything, seeing he himself giveth to all life, and breath, and all things; and he made of one every nation of men to dwell on all the face of the earth, having determined their appointed seasons, and the bounds of their habitation; that they should seek God, if haply, they might feel after him and find him, though he is not far from each one of us; for in him we live, and move, and have our being; as certain even of your own poets have said, For we are also his offspring.—Acts 17:22-28.

Consider the meaning of the fact that prayer and worship are thus universal; that all peoples do "seek God, if haply, they might feel after him and find him." It is said that an ignorant African woman, after hearing her first Christian sermon, remarked to her neighbor, "There! I always told you that there ought to be a God like that." Somewhere in every man there is the capacity for worship and prayer, for the apprehension of God and the love of him. Is not this the distinctive quality of man and the noblest faculty which he possesses? How then are we treating this best of our endowments?

O Lord our God, grant us grace to desire Thee with our whole heart; that so desiring we may seek and find Thee; and so finding Thee may love Thee; and loving Thee, may hate those sins from which Thou hast redeemed us. Amen.—Anselm (1033-1109).

Third Day, First Week

Prayer has been greatly discredited in the minds of many by its use during war. Men have felt the absurdity of praying on opposite sides of a battle, of making God a tribal leader in heaven, to give victory, as Zeus and Apollo used to do, to their favorites. Let us grant all the narrow, bitter, irrational elements that thus appear in prayer during a war, but let us not be blind to the meaning of this momentous fact: *whenever in national life a time of great stress comes, men, however sceptical, feel the impulse to pray.* How natural is Hezekiah's cry in the siege of Jerusalem!

O Jehovah, the God of Israel, that sittest above the cherubim, thou art the God, even thou alone, of all the kingdoms of the earth; thou hast made heaven and earth. Incline thine ear, O Jehovah, and hear; open thine eyes, O Jehovah, and see; and hear the words of Sennacherib, wherewith he hath sent him to defy the living God. Of a truth, Jehovah, the kings of Assyria have laid waste the nations and their lands, and have cast their gods into the fire; for they were no gods but the work of men's hands, wood and stone; therefore they have destroyed them. Now therefore, O Jehovah our God, save thou us, I beseech thee, out of his hand, that all the

**kingdoms of the earth may know that thou Jehovah art God alone.
—II Kings 19:15-19.**

Consider now the same tendency to pray in a crisis, which appears in the European war. Here is a passage from a Scotchman's letter, describing the infidel in his town, who never went to church, but who now sits in the kirk, and is moved to tears when he hears the minister pray for the king's forces, and for the bereaved at home: "It was then that my friend stifled a sob. There was Something after all, Something greater than cosmic forces, greater than law—with an eye to pity and an arm to save. There was God. My friend's son was with the famous regiment that was swaying to and fro, grappling with destiny. He was helpless—and there was only God to appeal to. There comes an hour in life when the heart realizes that instinct is mightier far than logic. With us in the parish churches of Scotland the great thing is the sermon. But today it is different; the great thing now is prayer." So always a crisis shakes loose the tendency to pray.

O Lord God of Hosts, grant to those who have gone forth to fight our battles by land or sea, protection in danger, patience in suffering, and moderation in victory. Look with compassion on the sick, the wounded, and the captives; sanctify to them their trials, and turn their hearts unto Thee. For Thy dear Son's sake, O Lord, pardon and receive the dying; have mercy upon the widow and fatherless, and comfort all who mourn. O gracious Father, who makest wars to cease in all the world, restore to us, Thy people, speedily the blessing of peace, and grant that our present troubles may be overruled to Thy glory, in the extension of the Redeemer's Kingdom, and the union of all nations in Thy faith, fear, and love. Hear, O Lord, and answer us; for Jesus Christ's sake. Amen.—
E. Hawkins (1789-1882).

Fourth Day, First Week

H. Clay Trumbull tells us that a soldier in the Civil War, wounded in a terrific battle at Fort Wagner, was asked by an army chaplain, "Do you ever pray?" "Sometimes," was the answer; "I prayed last Saturday night, when we were in that fight at Wagner. I guess everybody prayed *there*." Consider how inevitably the impulse to

pray asserts itself whenever critical danger comes suddenly upon
any life. In view of this, read the Psalmist's description of a storm at
sea:

They that go down to the sea in ships,
That do business in great waters;
These see the works of Jehovah,
And his wonders in the deep.
For he commandeth, and raiseth the stormy wind,
Which lifteth up the waves thereof.
They mount up to the heavens, they go down again to the depths:
Their soul melteth away because of trouble.
They reel to and fro, and stagger like a drunken man,
And are at their wits' end.
Then they cry unto Jehovah in their trouble.

—Psalm 107:23-28.

Remember those times in your experience or observation when
either you or someone else has been thrown back by an emergency
upon this natural tendency to pray in a crisis. Consider what it
means that this impulse to pray is not simply age-long and universal;
that it also is exhibited in every one of us—at least occasionally.
How natural as well as how noble is this prayer of Bishop Ridley
during the imprisonment that preceded his burning at the stake!

*O Heavenly Father, the Father of all wisdom, understanding, and
true strength, I beseech Thee, for Thy only Son our Savior Christ's
sake, look mercifully upon me, wretched creature, and send Thine
Holy Spirit into my breast; that not only I may understand according to Thy wisdom, how this temptation is to be borne off, and with
what answer it is to be beaten back; but also, when I must join to
fight in the field for the glory of Thy name, that then I, being
strengthened with the defence of Thy right hand, may manfully
stand in the confession of Thy faith, and of Thy truth, and may
continue in the same unto the end of my life, through the same our
Lord Jesus Christ. Amen.*—Bishop Ridley (1500-1555).

Fifth Day, First Week

The instinctive turning of the heart to a "Power not ourselves" is
often felt, not alone in crises of peril, but in the presence of great

responsibility, for which a man unaided feels inadequate. Despite Solomon's shallowness of life, there were times when something finer and deeper was revealed in him than his deeds would have suggested. When he first realized that the new responsibility of kingship was upon him, how elevated the spirit of his impulsive prayer!

And now, O Jehovah my God, thou hast made thy servant king instead of David my father: and I am but a little child; I know not how to go out or come in. And thy servant is in the midst of thy people which thou hast chosen, a great people, that cannot be numbered nor counted for multitude. Give thy servant therefore an understanding heart to judge thy people, that I may discern between good and evil; for who is able to judge this thy great people? —I Kings 3:7-9.

As a companionpiece with this cry of Solomon, see Lincoln's revealing words: "I have been driven many times to my knees by the overwhelming conviction that I had nowhere else to go; my own wisdom and that of all around me seemed insufficient for the day." Whenever a man faces tasks for which he feels inadequate and upon whose accomplishment much depends, he naturally turns to prayer. Let us imagine ourselves in Luther's place, burdened with new and crushing responsibilities, and facing powerful enemies, when he cried:

O Thou, my God! Do Thou, my God, stand by me, against all the world's wisdom and reason. Oh, do it! Thou must do it! Yea, Thou alone must do it! Not mine, but Thine, is the cause. For my own self, I have nothing to do with these great and earthly lords. I would prefer to have peaceful days, and to be out of this turmoil. But Thine, O Lord, is this cause; it is righteous and eternal. Stand by me, Thou true Eternal God! In no man do I trust. All that is of the flesh and savours of the flesh is here of no account. God, O God! dost Thou not hear me, O my God? Art Thou dead? No. Thou canst not die; Thou art only hiding Thyself. Hast Thou chosen me for this work? I ask Thee how I may be sure of this, if it be Thy will; for I would never have thought, in all my life, of undertaking aught against such great lords. Stand by me, O God, in the Name of Thy dear Son, Jesus Christ, who shall be my Defence and Shelter, yea, my Mighty Fortress, through the might and strength of Thy Holy Spirit. God help me. Amen.—Martin Luther (1483-1546).

Sixth Day, First Week

And when Daniel knew that the writing was signed, he went into his house (now his windows were open in his chamber toward Jerusalem); and he kneeled upon his knees three times a day, and prayed, and gave thanks before his God, as he did aforetime.—Daniel 6:10.

We are evidently dealing here with a new element in prayer, not apparent in our previous discussion. *Prayer, to Daniel, was not simply an impulsive cry of need, wrung from him by sudden crises or by overwhelming responsibilities.* Daniel had done with the impulse to pray what all wise people do with the impulse to eat. They do not neglect it until imperious hunger demands it to save their lives or until special work absolutely forces them to it. They rather recognize eating as a normal need of human beings, to be met regularly. So Daniel not only prayed in emergencies of peril and responsibility; he prayed three times a day. How many of us leave the instinct of prayer dormant until a crisis calls it into activity! "Jehovah, in *trouble* have they visited thee; they poured out a prayer *when thy chastening was upon them*" (Isaiah 26:16). Consider how inadequate such a use of prayer is.

I am forced, good Father, to seek Thee daily, and Thou offerest Thyself daily to be found: whensoever I seek, I find Thee, in my house, in the fields, in the temple, and in the highway. Whatsoever I do, Thou art with me; whether I eat or drink, whether I write or work, go to ride, read, meditate, or pray, Thou art ever with me; wheresoever I am, or whatsoever I do, I feel some measure of Thy mercies and love. If I be oppressed, Thou defendest me: if I be envied, Thou guardest me; if I hunger, Thou feedest me; whatsoever I want Thou givest me. O continue this Thy loving-kindness towards me for ever, that all the world may see Thy power, Thy mercy, and Thy love, wherein Thou hast not failed me, and even my enemies shall see that Thy mercies endure forever.—J. Norden (1548-1625).

Seventh Day, First Week

For this cause I bow my knees unto the Father, from whom every family in heaven and on earth is named, that he would grant

you, according to the riches of his glory, that ye may be strengthened with power through his Spirit in the inward man; that Christ
may dwell in your hearts through faith; to the end that ye, being
rooted and grounded in love, may be strong to apprehend with all
the saints what is the breadth and length and height and depth, and
to know the love of Christ which passeth knowledge, that ye may
be filled unto all the fulness of God.—Eph. 3:14-19.

Compare praying like this with the spasmodic cry of occasional
need and see how great the difference is. Here prayer has risen into
an elevated demand on life, unselfish and constant. It gathers up the
powers of the soul in a constraining desire for God's blessing on the
one who prays and on all men. What starts in the pagan as an un-
regulated and fitful impulse has become in Paul an intelligent, per-
severing, and well-directed habit. As power of thought confused and
weak in an Australian aboriginal, becomes in a Newton capable of
grasping laws that hold the stars together, so prayer may begin in the
race or in the individual as an erratic and ineffective impulse, but
may grow to be a dependable and saving power. Consider how
much you understand this latent force in your own life and how
effectively you are using it.

*O God, Thou art Life, Wisdom, Truth, Bounty, and Blessedness,
the Eternal, the only true Good! My God and my Lord, Thou art
my hope and my heart's joy. I confess, with thanksgiving, that Thou
hast made me in Thine image, that I may direct all my thoughts to
Thee, and love Thee. Lord, make me to know Thee aright, that I
may more and more love, and enjoy, and possess Thee. And since,
in the life here below, I cannot fully attain this blessedness, let it at
least grow in me day by day, until it all be fulfilled at last in the life
to come. Here be the knowledge of Thee increased, and there let it
be perfected. Here let my love to Thee grow, and there let it ripen;
that my joy being here great in hope, may there in fruition be made
perfect. Amen.*—Anselm (1033-1109).

COMMENT FOR THE WEEK

I

When any one undertakes to study the meaning and to cultivate
the habit of prayer, it is well for him to understand from the begin-

ning that he is dealing with a natural function of his life and not with an artificial addition. Raising palm trees in Greenland would be an unnatural proceeding. They never were intended to grow there, and never can grow there save under stress of artificial forcing. The culture of prayer would be just as strained a procedure, were it not true that the tendency to pray is native to us, that prayer is indigenous in us, that we *do* pray, one way or another, even though fitfully and without effect, and that men always have prayed and always will pray. The definition of man as a "praying animal," while not comprehensive, is certainly correct. *The culture of prayer, therefore, is not importing an alien, but is training a native citizen of the soul.* Professor William James of Harvard was thinking of this when he wrote: "We hear in these days of scientific enlightenment a great deal of discussion about the efficacy of prayer; and many reasons are given us why we should not pray, whilst others are given us why we should. But in all this very little is said of the reason why we do pray. . . . The reason why we do pray is simply that we cannot help praying."

Our justification for calling prayer natural may be found, in part, in the *universality* of it. In some form or other, it is found everywhere, in all ages and among all peoples. The most discouraging circumstances do not crush it, and theories of the universe directly antagonistic do not prevent it. Buddhism, a religion theoretically without a God, ought logically to exclude prayer; but in countries where Buddhism is dominant, prayer is present. Confucius, a good deal of an agnostic, urged his disciples not to have much to do with the gods; and today Confucius is himself a god and millions worship him. *Before the tendency to pray all barriers go down.*

The traveler climbs the foothills of the Himalayas, and among the Khonds of North India hears the prayer: "O Lord, we know not what is good for us. Thou knowest what it is. For it we pray." The archeologist goes back among the Aztec ruins and reads their prayer in affliction: "O merciful Lord, let this chastisement with which thou hast visited us, give us freedom from evil and from folly." The historian finds the Greek world typical of all ancient civilizations at least in this, that prayer is everywhere. Xenophon begins each day's march with prayer; Pericles begins every address with prayer; the greatest of Greek orations, Demosthenes' "On the Crown," and the greatest of Greek poems, "The Iliad," are opened with prayer. When from the superstitious habits of the populace one turns to the most elevated and philosophic spirits to see what they will say, he hears Plato, "Every man of sense before beginning an important work will ask help of the gods." And turning from Plato's preaching to his practice, he reads this beautiful petition, "King Zeus, grant us the good whether we pray for it or not, but evil keep from us, though we pray for it."

If today one crosses the borders of Christianity into Mohammedanism, not only will he find formal prayer five times daily, when the muezzin calls, but he will read descriptions of prayer like this from a Sufi—"There are three degrees in prayer. The first is when it is only spoken by the lips. The second is when with difficulty, by a resolute effort, the soul succeeds in fixing its thought on divine things. The third is when the soul finds it hard to turn away from God." And if from all others, one looks to the Hebrew people, with what unanimous ascription do they say, "O thou that hearest prayer, unto thee shall all flesh come" (Psa. 65:2) A man is cutting himself off from one of the elemental functions of human life when he denies in himself the tendency to pray.

II

Moreover, justification for calling prayer natural is found in the fact that *mankind never outgrows prayer*. Both the practice and the theory of it have proved infinitely adaptable to all stages of culture. In its lowest forms, among the most savage peoples, prayer and magic were indistinguishable. To pray then was to use charms that compelled the assent of the gods. And from such pagan beginnings to Jesus in the Garden or a modern scientist upon his knees, prayer, like all other primary functions, has proved capable of unlimited development. It has not been crushed but has been lifted into finer forms by spiritual and intellectual advance. It has shaped its course like a river, to the banks of each generation's thought; but it has flowed on, fed from fountains that changing banks do not affect. Nowhere is this more plain than in the Bible. Compare the dying prayer of Samson, as he wound his arms around the sustaining pillars of the Philistine dining hall and cried: "O Lord Jehovah, remember me, I pray thee, and strengthen me, I pray thee, only this once, O God, that I may be at once avenged of the Philistines for my two eyes" (Judges 16:28); with the dying prayer of Stephen, as he was being stoned, "Lord, lay not this sin to their charge" (Acts

7:60). Both are prayers, but they come from two ages between which the revelation of God and the meaning of prayer had infinitely widened.

Both in the Scripture and out of it, the quality of prayer is suited to the breadth or narrowness of view, the generosity or bitterness of spirit, which the generation or the individual possesses. As Sabatier puts it, *"The history of prayer is the history of religion."* At one end of the scale,

> "In even savage bosoms
> There are longings, yearnings, strivings
> For the good they comprehend not;
> And their feeble hands and helpless,
> Groping blindly in the darkness,
> Touch God's right hand in that darkness
> And are lifted up and strengthened."

At the other end of the scale, Coleridge says, "The act of praying is the very highest energy of which the human mind is capable"; and President Harper of the University of Chicago, on his death-bed prays: "May there be for me a life beyond this life; and in that life may there be work to do, tasks to accomplish. If in any way a soul has been injured or a friend hurt, may the harm be overcome, if it is possible." The human soul never outgrows prayer. At their lowest, men pray crudely, ignorantly, bitterly; at their best, men pray intelligently, spiritually, magnanimously. *Prayer is not only universal in extent; it is infinite in quality.* A man may well give himself to the deepening and purifying of his prayer, for it is as natural in human life as thought.

III

The naturalness of prayer is further seen in the fact that *prayer is latent in the life of every one of us.* At first the experience of some may seem to gainsay this. They have given up praying. They get on very well without it, and when they are entirely candid they confess that they disbelieve in it. But they must also confess that their disbelief lies in their *opinions* and not in their *impulses.* When some overwhelming need comes upon them, their impulse is still to pray.

Modern scepticism has done all that it could to make prayer unreasonable. It has viewed the world as a machine, regular as an automaton, uncontrollable as sunrise. It has made whatever God there is a prisoner in the laws of his own world, powerless to assist his children. It has denied everything that makes prayer possible; and yet men, having believed all that sceptical thought says, still have their times of prayer. Like water in an artesian well, walled up by modern concrete, prayer still seeps through, it breaks out; nature is stronger than artifice, and streams flowing underground in our lives insist on finding vent. Sometimes a crisis of personal danger lets loose this hidden impulse. "I hadn't prayed in ten years," the writer heard a railroad man exclaim when his train had just escaped a wreck; "but I prayed *then*." Sometimes a crushing responsibility makes men pray almost in spite of themselves. General Kodoma, of the Japanese army during the Russian war, used to retire each morning for an hour of prayer. When asked the reason, he answered: "When a man has done everything in his power, there remains nothing but the help of the gods." Anything—peril, responsibility, anxiety, grief—that shakes us out of our mere opinions, down into our native impulses, is likely to make us pray.

This is true of whole populations as well as of individuals. Shall not a war like the appalling conflict in Europe make men doubt God and disbelieve all good news of him that they have heard? Only of far distant spectators is any such reaction true. In the midst of the crisis itself, where the burdens of sacrifice are being borne and super-human endurance, courage, and selflessness are required, the reaction of men, as all observers note, is accurately described in Cardinal Mercier's famous pastoral letter: "Men long unaccustomed to prayer are turning again to God. Within the army, within the civil world, in public, and within the individual conscience there is prayer. Nor is that prayer today a word learned by rote, uttered lightly by the lip; it surges from the troubled heart, it takes the form at the feet of God of the very sacrifice of life." Whether in the individual or in society, great shocks that loosen the foundations of human life and let the primal tendencies surge up, always set free the pent fountains of prayer. *In the most sceptical man or generation prayer is always underground, waiting.* Henry Ward Beecher was giving us something more than a whimsical simile when he said: "I pray on the principle that the wine knocks the cork out of a bottle. There is an inward fermentation and there must be a vent." Even Comte, with his system of religion that utterly banished God, soul, and immortality, prescribed for his disciples two hours of prayer daily, because he recognized the act itself as one of the elemental functions of human nature.

Whether, therefore, we consider the universality of prayer, or its infinite adaptability to all stages of culture and intelligence, or the fact that it is latent in every one of us, we come to the same conclusion: praying is a natural activity of human life. We may only note in passing the patent argument here for the truth of religion. *Can it be that all men, in all ages and all lands, have been engaged in "talking forever to a silent world from which no answer comes"?* If we can be sure of anything, is it not this—that wherever a human function has persisted, unwearied by time, uncrushed by disappointment, rising to noblest form and finest use in the noblest and finest souls, that function corresponds with some Reality? Hunger never could have persisted without food, nor breathing without air, nor intellectual life without truth, nor prayer without God. Burke said that it was difficult to press an indictment against a nation. It is far more difficult to sustain a charge against all mankind.

IV

From this argument which the naturalness of prayer suggests, we press on, however, to a matter more immediate to our purpose. The fact that prayer is one of our native tendencies accounts for one peril in our use of it. *We let prayer be merely a tendency, and therefore spasmodic, occasional, untrained.* A tragedy is always present in any fine function of human nature that is left undisciplined. The impulse to love is universal; but left to be merely an impulse, it is brutal and fleshly. The love that inspires our noblest poems and is celebrated in our greatest music, that builds Christian homes and makes family life beautiful, is a primal impulse trained and elevated, become intelligent, disciplined, and consecrated. The tendency to think is universal, but left as such, it is but the wayward and futile intellect of savages. Their powers of thinking are stagnant, called into activity by accident, not well understood, carefully trained, and intelligently exercised. So prayer left to spasmodic use is a futile thing. In the one hundred and seventh Psalm, a marvelous description of a storm at sea ends with a verse which reveals the nature of impulsive prayer: "They . . . are at their wits' end. Then they cry unto Jehovah" (Psalm 107:27, 28). When prayer is left untrained, men pray only when they have reached their wits' end. In moments of extreme physical danger, men who never make a daily friend of God, cry to him in their need. "He that will learn to pray," says George Herbert, pithily, "let him go to sea"; and Shakespeare in the "Tempest," knowing human nature as the Psalmist knew it, has the sailors, when the storm breaks, cry: "All lost! To prayers! To prayers! All lost!" In extreme moral danger, also, where pleasant dalliance with evil has run out into the unbreakable habit of evil, men almost always pray. And in death how naturally men think of God! So Dame Quickly says of the dying Falstaff: "Now I, to comfort him, bid him a' should not think of God. I hoped there was no need to trouble himself with any such thoughts yet!"

Prayer, left as an undisciplined impulse, inevitably sinks into such a spasmodic and frantic use. "When my soul fainted within me, I remembered Jehovah" (Jonah 2:7). Like the old Greek dramatists, men hopelessly tangle the plot of their lives, until at the end, with a dilemma insoluble by human ingenuity and power, they swing a god from the wings by machinery to disentangle the desperate situation. They use prayer as a *deus-ex-machina*, a last resort when they are in extremity. In one way or another, how many of us must accuse ourselves of this fitful use of prayer! One of the supreme powers of our lives is left to the control of impulse and accident, its nature unstudied, and its exercise untrained.

v

The baneful effect of this spasmodic use of prayer is easily seen. *For one thing it utterly neglects all Christian conceptions of God and goes back to the pagan thought of him. God becomes nothing more than a power to be occasionally called in to our help.* This is the conception of an Indian woman bowing at an idol's shrine. Her god is power, mysterious and masterful, whose help she seeks in her emergencies. When, therefore, we pray as she does, fitfully running to God in occasional crises, we are going back in substance, if not in form, to paganism. We deserve Luther's rebuke in his sermon on praying to the saints: "We honor them and call upon them only when we have a pain in our legs or our heads, or when our pockets are empty." But the best of humanity have traveled a long way from such an idea of deity. The Christian God desires to be to every one an inward and abiding friend, a purifying presence in daily life, the One whose moral purpose continually restrains and whose love upholds. Above all advances made in human life none is so significant as this advance in the thought of God. We have moved from rumbling oxcarts to limited express trains, from mud huts to cathedrals, from tom-toms to orchestras. If we neglected these gains, we should rightly be regarded as strange anachronisms. Yet in our treatment of God how often are we ancient pagans born after our time! We are examples of religious reversal to type. We are misdated A. D. instead of B. C. when we use God as a power to be occasionally summoned to our aid.

Consider a new parable of a father and his two sons. One son looked upon his father as a last resort in critical need. He never came to him for friendly conference, never sought his advice, in little difficulties never was comforted by his help. He did not make his father his confidant. He went to college and wrote home only when he wanted money. He fell into disgrace, and called on his father only when he needed legal aid. He ran his life with utter disregard of his father's character or purpose, and turned to him only when in desperate straits. The other son saw in his father's love the supreme motive of his life. He was moved by daily gratitude so that to be well-pleasing to his father was his joy and his ideal. His father was his friend. He confided in him, was advised by him, kept close to him, and in *his* crises came to his father with a naturalness born of long habit, like Jesus, who having prayed without ceasing, now at last bows in Gethsemane. *Is there any doubt as to which is the nobler sonship? And is not the former type a true picture of our relationship with God when we leave prayer to be a merely instinctive and untrained cry of need?*

VI

For another thing, this use of prayer as merely a spasmodic cry out of an occasional crisis, makes it utterly selfish. We think of God solely with reference to our own emergencies. We never remember the Most High except when we wish him to run an errand for us. Our prayer does not concern itself with the fulfilment of his great purposes in us and in the world, and does not relate itself to a life devoted to his will. In utter selfishness we forget God until it occurs to us that we may get something from him.

Some men treat God in this respect as others treat their country. That regard for native land which in some has inspired heroic and sacrificial deeds, appears in others in the disguise of utter selfishness. Consider a man who does nothing whatever for his country; is not interested in her problems; is careless of the franchise, evades every public responsibility, and even dodges taxes. One would suppose that this man never thought of his country at all. Upon the contrary, there are occasions when he thinks of her at once. When his person or property is attacked and his rights invaded, this same man will appeal clamorously to the government for protection. He reserves every thought of his country for the hours of personal crisis. His relationship with his government is exhausted in spasmodic cries for help. *He furnishes a true parallel to that ignoble type of religion, in which prayer, left fitful and undisciplined, is nothing more than an occasional, selfish demand on God.*

VII

The shame of leaving thus uncultivated one of the noblest functions of man's spirit is emphasized when we face the testimony of the masters in prayer concerning its possibilities. What the power of thought can mean must be seen in the thinkers; what prayer can do must be seen in the pray-ers. Whenever *they* speak, language seems to them inadequate to describe the saving and empowering influences of habitual prayer. As in our Christian songs, where we leave the more superficial differences of opinion and go down into the essential spirit of worship, Catholics and Protestants, Jews and Gentiles, men of every shade of special belief and sectarian alliance are authors of the hymns we all sing, so in prayer men of opposite opinions agree as one. Luther, the Protestant, is alien at how many points from St. Bernard the Catholic, and yet says Luther—"In the faith wherein St. Bernard prays, do I pray also." Not only does a liberal philosopher, Sabatier, say, "Prayer is religion in act; that is, prayer is real religion"; and a conservative theologian, Hartmann, say, "God has given to real prayer the power to shape the future for men and the world"; and a Catholic poet, Francis Thompson, say, "Prayer is the very sword of the saints": even Professor Tyndall, the scientist, who was regarded by the Christians of his generation as the most aggressive antagonist of prayer, says: "It is not my habit of mind to think otherwise than solemnly of the feelings which prompt to prayer. Often unreasonable, even contemptible, in its purer forms prayer hints at disciplines which few of us can neglect without moral loss." If there is any element in human life to whose inestimable value we have abundant testimony, it is prayer; and to leave misunderstood and untrained a power capable of such high uses is a spiritual tragedy.

This, then, is the summary of the matter. Deep in every one of us lies the tendency to pray. If we allow it to remain merely a tendency, it becomes nothing but a selfish, unintelligent, occasional cry of need. But understood and disciplined, it reveals possibilities whose limits never have been found.

SUGGESTIONS FOR THOUGHT AND DISCUSSION

How far can prayer be said to be natural to all peoples in all times?

Are the following exercises forms of prayer?

An African throwing a stone on the votive pile along the roadside.

A Buddhist using a prayer wheel.

A Thibetan tying a prayer flag to a tree.

An Indian Fakir lying on a bed of spikes.

An American nailing a horse shoe over the door for good luck.

How far can superstitious prayers, growing out of ignorance, of mysterious happenings and attempts to propitiate some unknown mighty power, be said to be proof of the universality of prayer?

How far can Paul's statement in regard to the men of Athens being very religious be duplicated in non-Christian countries today?

To what degree is crying out for help in time of great trouble a proof that prayer is natural? Was Stephen's prayer as natural as Samson's? Compare Hezekiah's prayer at the siege of Jerusalem with prayer in modern wars. Is the Psalmist's description of a man praying in a storm at sea proof of the naturalness of prayer?

Is prayer more natural to some types of individuals and races than others? Is it more natural to women than men?

In the sense that you use the word "prayer," do all men pray?

How far is the universality of prayer a proof of its reality?

What effect has lack of control and training upon fine natural tendencies?

Is love involuntary, or can a man control and develop his love instinct?

To what degree is the instinct to pray capable of development and direction?

Wherein do untrained natural prayer instincts fall short? Why are the prayers of a Christian often really pagan in character?

What were the distinctive elements in Daniel's prayer? in the prayer of Ephesians 3:14-19?

Can spasmodic and untrained prayer be unselfish?

How can prayer be trained? What determines the limit of the development of prayer in any individual? For instance, what process is necessary to develop the turning of a prayer wheel into a prayer like Stephen's?

CHAPTER II

Prayer as Communion with God

DAILY READINGS

First Day, Second Week

The thought of prayer as a natural function in human life ought to be of this practical service to us: it should keep us from yielding too easily to disbelief or discouragement when we have difficulty with prayer in our individual experience. At least, so one of the psalmists felt.

My God, my God, why hast thou forsaken me?
Why art thou so far from helping me, and from the words of my
    groaning?
O my God, I cry in the daytime, but thou answerest not;
And in the night season, and am not silent.
But thou art holy,
O thou that inhabitest the praises of Israel.
Our fathers trusted in thee:
They trusted, and thou didst deliver them.
They cried unto thee, and were delivered:
They trusted in thee, and were not put to shame.
                      —Psalm 22:1-5.

Note the three troubles which this psalmist has been having with prayer. He cannot make God seem real to him; his prayer brings him no relief in his difficulties; and even persistency in prayer accomplishes nothing. Then he remembers that prayer is not something with which he, for the first time in history, is experimenting. "Our fathers trusted in thee . . . and thou didst deliver them." He sees that the accumulating testimony of his fathers in all ages

bears witness to the power of prayer. He therefore sensibly concludes
that he would better not pit a few months of individual failure in
praying against the general experience of the race. In view of what
prayer has meant to all peoples, *he sees that probably the trouble is
with himself and not with prayer.* He sets himself therefore to
understand prayer if he can, and in the 22nd verse of the Psalm, he
begins the recital of the victorious outcome: "I will declare thy
name unto my brethren: In the midst of the assembly will I praise
thee." May God make us as sensible as this psalmist and give us as
real a triumph!

*O God, who art, and wast, and art to come, before whose face the
generations rise and pass away; age after age the living seek Thee,
and find that of Thy faithfulness there is no end. Our fathers in
their pilgrimage walked by Thy guidance, and rested on Thy compassion; still to their children be Thou the cloud by day, the fire by
night. In our manifold temptations, Thou alone knowest and are
ever nigh: in sorrow, Thy pity revives the fainting soul; in our prosperity and ease, it is Thy Spirit only that can wean us from our pride
and keep us low. O Thou sole Source of peace and righteousness!
take now the veil from every heart; and join us in one communion
with Thy prophets and saints who have trusted in Thee, and were
not ashamed. Not of our worthiness, but of Thy tender mercy, hear
our prayer. Amen.*—James Martineau (1805-1900).

Second Day, Second Week

*Let us consider this week some of the practical reasons for our
failure to make the most out of our power to pray.* To that end read
these verses representing two aspects of the Master's life:

We must work the works of him that sent me, while it is day:
the night cometh, when no man can work.—John 9:4.

In the morning, a great while before day, he rose up and went
out, and departed into a desert place, and there prayed.—Mark
1:35.

Which of these two emphases in the Christian life do we appreciate the better? Is it not clear that all the characteristic en-
thusiasms of our day cluster around work? In the churches, service
is the popular note, and the favorite hymns are "The Son of God

goes forth to war," "Soldiers of Christ arise," and their kind. Our failure in prayer is partly due to the prevailing temper of our generation, which in its splendid enthusiasm for work has neglected that culture of prayer, on which in the end the finest quality of spirit and the deepest resources of power must depend. Is not this one reason why keen observers note that our generation is marked by practical efficiency and spiritual shallowness? May we not hope to keep in ourselves the best gains of this efficient age and at the same time recover the "practice of the presence of God"?

Almighty Father, enter Thou our hearts, and so fill us with Thy love, that, forsaking all evil desires, we may embrace Thee, our only good. Show unto us, for Thy mercies' sake, O Lord our God, what Thou art unto us. Say unto our souls, I am thy salvation. So speak that we may hear. Our hearts are before Thee; open Thou our ears; let us hasten after Thy voice, and take hold on Thee. Hide not Thy face from us, we beseech Thee, O Lord. Enlarge Thou the narrowness of our souls, that Thou mayest enter in. Repair the ruinous mansions, that Thou mayest dwell there. Hear us, O Heavenly Father, for the sake of Thine only Son, Jesus Christ, our Lord, who liveth and reigneth with Thee and the Holy Spirit, now and for ever. Amen.—St. Augustine (354-430).

Third Day, Second Week

Failure to cultivate our power of prayer goes back in many to childish ideas of prayer's meaning, which, never altogether outgrown, hamper us and make our praying seem unreasonable and futile. There are some who still think of prayer in terms of childish supplications to a divine Santa Claus. Let us note the two aspects of truth set forth in these two passages:

And he sat down, and called the twelve; and he saith unto them, If any man would be first, he shall be last of all, and servant of all. And he took a little child, and set him in the midst of them: and taking him in his arms, he said unto them, Whosoever shall receive one of such little children in my name, receiveth me: and whosoever receiveth me, receiveth not me, but him that sent me.—Mark 9:35-37.

When I was a child, I spake as a child, I felt as a child, I thought

as a child: now that I am become a man, I have put away childish
things.—I Cor. 13:11.

When Christ sets as our ideal the childlike qualities of sincerity
and humility, he is not asking us to be *childish.* Many foolish prayers
are offered by the well-meaning but unintelligent with the excuse
that they are childlike in their simple trust. But we are grown-up
children, and have an obligation to exercise our intelligence, to out-
grow infantile ideas of prayer that belittle it, and to enlarge our
conceptions of the significance which fellowship with God may have
for life. To pray to God as though he were Santa Claus is *childish;*
but a man may still be *childlike* in his faith and range up into another sort of praying:

> "Thou Life within my life, than self more near,
> Thou Veiled Presence infinitely clear;
> From all illusive shows of sense I flee
> To find my center and my rest in Thee."

*O Heavenly Father, the Author and Fountain of all truth, the
bottomless Sea of all understanding, send, we beseech Thee, Thy
Holy Spirit into our hearts, and lighten our understandings with
the beams of Thy heavenly grace. We ask this, O merciful Father,
for Thy dear Son, our Saviour, Jesus Christ's sake. Amen.*—Bishop
Ridley (1500-1555).

Fourth Day, Second Week

Childishness in prayer is chiefly evidenced in an overweening
desire to beg *things* from God, and a corresponding failure to desire
above all else the *friendship of God himself.* The same growth ought
to take place in our relationship with God which occurs in a normal
fellowship between a child and his parents. At first the child wants
the parents' gifts, and thinks of the parents largely in terms of the
things which they do for his comfort and pleasure. He is not able
yet to appreciate the value of the parents' personalities. A sure sign
of wholesome maturity, however, is found in the child's deepening
understanding of the parents themselves—his increasing delight in
their friendship, thankfulness for their care, acceptance of their
ideals, reliance on their counsel, and joy in their approval. The child

grows through desiring things from his parents into love of his parents, for their own sakes.

A certain man had two sons: and the younger of them said to his father, Father, give me the portion of thy substance that falleth to me. And he divided unto them his living. And not many days after, the younger son gathered all together and took his journey into a far country; and there he wasted his substance with riotous living. . . . But when he came to himself he said, How many hired servants of my father's have bread enough and to spare, and I perish here with hunger! I will arise and go to my father, and will say unto him, Father, I have sinned against heaven, and in thy sight: I am no more worthy to be called thy son: make me as one of thy hired servants.—Luke 15:11-13, 17-19.

Note the change of prayer from *"Give me"* to *"Make me."* Whether through experience of sin or sorrow or hard practical struggle we come to a real maturity, we always tend to grow out of crying to God "Give me" into the deeper prayer "Make me." In a word we cease valuing God merely because of the things he may give, and we come into the love of God himself and the desire to be made over by him.

Grant me, O most loving Lord, to rest in Thee above all creatures, above all health and beauty, above all glory and honor, above all power and dignity, above all knowledge and subtilty, above all riches and art, above all fame and praise, above all sweetness and comfort, above all hope and promise, above all gifts and favors that Thou canst give and impart to us, above all jubilee that the mind of man can receive and feel; finally, above angels and archangels, and above all the heavenly host, above all things visible and invisible, and above all that Thou art not, O my God. It is too small and unsatisfying, whatsoever Thou bestowest on me apart from Thee, or revealest to me, or promisest, whilst Thou art not seen, and not fully obtained. For surely my heart cannot truly rest, nor be entirely contented, unless it rest in Thee. Amen.—Thomas à Kempis (1379-1471).

Fifth Day, Second Week

Prayer has failed in some because it has always appeared to them as an *obligation rather than a privilege.* When they think of it they think of a duty to be done. Contrast with this the glowing words of the sixty-third Psalm:

O God, thou art my God; earnestly will I seek thee: . . .
Because thy lovingkindness is better than life,
My lips shall praise thee. . . .
My soul shall be satisfied as with marrow and fatness;
And my mouth shall praise thee with joyful lips;
When I remember thee upon my bed,
And meditate on thee in the night-watches.
For thou hast been my help,
And in the shadow of thy wings will I rejoice.
My soul followeth hard after thee:
Thy right hand upholdeth me.—Psalm 63:1, 3, 5-8.

Prayer here is not a burden to be borne, an obligation to be fulfilled, something that is due to God and must be paid. Prayer is a *privilege;* like friendship and family love and laughter, great books, great music, and great art, it is one of life's opportunities to be grasped thankfully and used gladly. The man who misses the deep meanings of prayer has not so much refused an obligation; he has robbed himself of life's supreme privilege—friendship with God.

O Thou divine Spirit that, in all events of life, art knocking at the door of my heart, help me to respond to Thee. I would not be driven blindly as the stars over their courses. I would not be made to work out Thy will unwillingly, to fulfil Thy law unintelligently, to obey Thy mandates unsympathetically. I would take the events of my life as good and perfect gifts from Thee; I would receive even the sorrows of life as disguised gifts from Thee. I would have my heart open at all times to receive—at morning, noon, and night; in spring, and summer, and winter. Whether Thou comest to me in sunshine or in rain, I would take Thee into my heart joyfully. Thou art Thyself more than the sunshine, Thou art Thyself compensation for the rain; it is Thee and not Thy gifts I crave; knock, and I shall open unto Thee. Amen.—George Matheson.

Sixth Day, Second Week

I exhort therefore, first of all, that supplications, prayers, intercessions, thanksgivings, be made for all men; for kings and all that are in high place; that we may lead a tranquil and quiet life in all godliness and gravity. This is good and acceptable in the sight of God our Saviour; who would have all men to be saved, and come to the knowledge of the truth. For there is one God, one mediator also between God and men, himself man, Christ Jesus. . . . I desire therefore that the men pray in every place, lifting up holy hands, without wrath and disputing.—I Tim. 2:1-5, 8.

Our failure to think of prayer as a privilege may be partly due to the fact that we can pray any time, "in every place." The door to prayer is open so continuously that we fail to avail ourselves of an opportunity which is always there. There are plenty of people in London who never have seen the inside of Westminster Abbey, partly because they could go there any day. Consider then the aptness of Austin Phelps' illustration: "In the vestibule of St. Peter's, at Rome, is a doorway, which is walled up and marked with a cross. It is opened but four times in a century. On Christmas Eve, once in twenty-five years, the Pope approaches it in princely state, with the retinue of cardinals in attendance, and begins the demolition of the door, by striking it three times with a silver hammer. When the passage is opened, the multitude pass into the nave of the cathedral, and up to the altar, by an avenue which the majority of them never entered thus before, and never will enter thus again. Imagine that the way to the Throne of Grace were like the Porta Sancta, inaccessible, save once in a quarter of a century. Conceive that it were now ten years since you, or I, or any other sinner, had been *permitted* to pray: and that fifteen long years must drag themselves away, before we could venture again to approach God; and that, at the most, we could not hope to pray more than two or three times in a lifetime! With what solicitude we should wait for the coming of that Holy Day!" It may be that through sheer negligence and the deceiving influence of good but weak intentions, we are missing one of life's great privileges, because it is so commonplace.

O Lord, keep me sensitive to the grace that is round about me. May the familiar not become neglected! May I see Thy goodness in my daily bread, and may the comfort of my home take my thoughts to the mercy seat of God!—J. H. Jowett.

Seventh Day, Second Week

Another practical reason for failure in prayer is found in *impatience*. We have made a few fitful and hurried attempts at praying and seeing no good consequence have impatiently called the practice worthless and have quit it. Suppose that a man should similarly make a dash at friendship and after throwing off a few trial conversations should dogmatically conclude that there was nothing in friendship after all. But friendship is not really tested in so dashing and occasional a way; friendship is rather a life to be lived, habitually, persistently—and its results are cumulative with the years. So prayer is a *cumulative life of friendship with God*.

And it came to pass, as he was praying in a certain place, that when he ceased, one of his disciples said unto him, Lord, teach us to pray, even as John also taught his disciples. And he said unto them, When ye pray, say, Father, Hallowed be thy name. Thy kingdom come. Give us day by day our daily bread. And forgive us our sins; for we ourselves also forgive every one that is indebted to us. And bring us not into temptation.—Luke 11:1-4.

Note that when the disciples heard Jesus pray they became aware that praying like his was nothing that they could happen on, or drift into, or dash off in a moment of special inspiration. Such praying was a lesson to be learned by assiduous practice. "It is a great art to commune with God," said Thomas à Kempis. We would not expect to take a try at a violin once in a while and yet make much of it. But see how we treat this finer instrument of prayer!

Which of these seven practical causes of failure, considered this week, apply to you?—pitting a little individual failure against the experience of the race; welcoming the emphasis on work to the exclusion of the emphasis on prayer; thinking of prayer childishly until it has seemed irrational; valuing God less than the things he may give until prayer has looked mean; regarding prayer as an obligation rather than a privilege; neglecting prayer because it is so familiar an opportunity; impatience with praying after a few, fitful trials.

Come, O Lord, in much mercy down into my soul, and take possession and dwell there. A homely mansion, I confess, for so glorious a Majesty, but such as Thou art fitting up for the reception of Thee,

●

by holy and fervent desires of Thine own inspiring. Enter then, and adorn, and make it such as Thou canst inhabit, since it is the work of Thy hands. Give me Thine own self, without which, though Thou shouldst give me all that ever Thou hast made, yet could not my desires be satisfied. Let my soul ever seek Thee, and let me persist in seeking, till I have found, and am in full possession of Thee. Amen.— St. Augustine (354-430).

COMMENT FOR THE WEEK

I

When a man begins to make earnest with prayer, desiring to see what can be done with it in his life, he finds that one of the first necessities is a fairly clear idea of what praying means. In most lives, behind all theoretical perplexities about this problem, there lies a practical experience with prayer that is very disconcerting.

When we were little children prayer was vividly real. We prayed with a naive confidence that we should obtain the things for which we asked. It made but little difference what the things were; for prayer was an Aladdin's lamp by rubbing which we summoned the angels of God to do our bidding, prayer was a blank check signed by the Almighty which we could fill in at will and present to the universe to be cashed. Such a conception of prayer is picturesquely revealed in the confession which Robertson of Brighton, the great English preacher, gives us in a paragraph about his childhood. "I remember when a very, very young boy," he says, "going out shooting with my father, and praying, as often as the dogs came to a point, that he might kill the bird. As he did not always do this, and as sometimes there would occur false points, my heart got bewildered. I believe I began to doubt sometimes the efficacy of prayer, sometimes the lawfulness of field sports. Once, too, I recollect when I was taken up with nine other boys at school to be unjustly punished, I prayed to escape the shame. The master previously to flogging all the others, said to me, to the great bewilderment of the whole school: 'Little boy, I excuse you: I have particular reasons for it,' and in fact, I was never flogged during the three years I was at that school. That incident settled my mind for a long time; only I doubt whether it did me any good, for prayer became a charm. I fancied myself the favorite of the Invisible. I knew that I carried about a talisman

unknown to others which would save me from all harm. It did not
make me better; it simply gave me security, as the Jew felt safe in
being the descendant of Abraham, or went into battle under the protection of the Ark, sinning no less all the time."

Many of us can look back to some such experience as this with
prayer; but, as with Robertson, serious doubts soon disturbed our
simple-hearted trust. How often we rubbed this magic lamp, and no
angels came! How steadily our faith in its efficacy gave place to
doubt and then to confident denial! As experience increased, we
relied not on prayer but on foresight, work, money, and shrewdness
to obtain our desires. Frederick Douglass said that in the days of his
slavery he used often to pray for freedom, but that his prayer was
not answered until it got down into his own heels and he ran away.
In that type of prayer we come increasingly to believe; but where
then, is the old trust that used to look for gifts from heaven? Indeed,
when in anguish we have cried for things on which the worth and
joy of life seemed utterly to depend, our faith has been staggered
by the impotence of our petition and the seeming indifference of
God. We have entered into Tennyson's crushing doubt:

> "O mother, praying God will save
> Thy sailor,—while thy head is bow'd,
> His heavy-shotted hammock-shroud
> Drops in his vast and wandering grave."

II

This practical disappointment with prayer as a means of getting
things leads in most men to one of two conclusions: either a man
gives over praying altogether; or else, continuing to pray, he seeks
a new motive for doing so to take the place of his old expectation
of definite results from God. Men used to put flowers on graves
because they thought that the departed spirits enjoyed the odor.
Although that superstition long has been overpassed, we still put
flowers on graves; but we have supplied a motive of sentiment in
place of the old realistic reason.

So men who learned to pray in childlike expectation of getting
precisely what they asked, are disillusioned by disappointment; but
they continue prayer, with a new motive. "Never mind if you do not
obtain your requests," men say in this second stage of their experi-

ence with prayer; "remember that it does *you* good to pray. The act itself enlarges your sympathies, quiets your mind, sweetens your disposition, widens the perspective of your thought. Give up all idea that some one does anything for you when you pray, but remember that you can do a great deal for yourself. In prayer we soothe our own spirits, calm our own anxieties, purify our own thoughts. Prayer is a helpful soliloquy; a comforting monologue; a noble form of auto-suggestion." So men returning disappointed from prayer as a means of obtaining definite requests, try to content themselves with prayer as *the reflex action of their own minds*. This is prayer's meaning, as they see it, put into an ancient parable: Two boys were sent into the fields to dig for hidden treasure, where all day they toiled in vain; and at evening, coming weary and disappointed home, they were met by their father. "After all," he said to comfort them, "you did get something—*the digging itself was good exercise*."

How many today think thus of prayer as a form of spiritual gymnastics—what Horace Bushnell called "mere dumb-bell exercise!" They lift the dumb-bell of intercessory prayer, not because they think it helps their friends, but because it strengthens the fiber of their own sympathy. They lift the dumb-bell of prayer for strength in temptation not because God helps them, but because the act itself steadies them. Prayer to them is one form of menticulture. But this kind of prayer is not likely to persist long. A thoughtful man balks at continuing to cry "O God," simply to improve the quality of his own voice. He shrinks from the process which Charles Kingsley describes in a letter as "Praying to oneself to change oneself; by which I mean the common method of trying by prayer to excite oneself into a state, a frame, an experience." Or if he does indulge in such spiritual exercise, he must call what he is doing by its right name; it is meditation, it is soliloquy, but it is not prayer. When a man indulges in this occasional self-communion for spiritual discipline; when no sense of fellowship with God is left in his soliloquies to remind one of Jesus' great confession, "I am not alone, but I and my Father" (John 8:16), his meditation can be called prayer only in the qualified phrase of one of the parables, where a man "stood and prayed . . . *with himself*" (Luke 18:11).

Is not this a typical experience of modern men? They find themselves impaled, as they think, upon the horns of a dilemma. *"Either,"* they say, *"prayer is an effective way of getting things by begging, or else prayer is merely the reflex action of a man's own mind."* But the *dilemma is false.* Prayer may involve something of both, but the heart of prayer is neither the one nor the other. The essential nature of prayer lies in a realm higher than either, where all that is false in both is transcended and all that is true is emphasized.

To Jesus, for example, the meaning of prayer was not that God would give him whatever he asked. God did not. That sustained and passionate petition where the Master thrice returned with blood-stained face, to cry, "Let this cup pass" (Matt. 26:39), had "No" for an answer. Neither did prayer mean to Jesus merely the reflex action of his own mind. Jesus prayed with such power that the one thing which his disciples asked him to teach them was how to pray (Luke 11:1); he prayed with such conscious joy that at times the very fashion of his countenance was changed with the glory of it (Luke 9:28, 29). Can you imagine him upon his knees then *talking to himself?* Was he merely catching the rebound of his own words? *Surely, when the Master prayed, he met somebody.* His life was impinged on by another Life. He felt "a Presence that disturbed him with the joy of elevated thoughts." His prayer was not monologue, but dialogue; not soliloquy, but friendship. *For prayer is neither chiefly begging for things, nor is it merely self-communion; it is that loftiest experience within the reach of any soul, communion with God.*

Of course, this does not answer all questions about prayer, nor exhaust all its meaning. Definite petition has its important place, and later we must consider it. *But at the beginning of our study, the thought of prayer as communion with God puts the center of the matter where it ought to be.* The great gift of God in prayer is himself, and whatever else he gives is incidental and secondary. Let us, then, consider in particular the significance which this truth has for our idea of praying.

III

For one thing, the thought of prayer as communion with God makes praying an *habitual attitude,* and not simply an *occasional act.* It is continuous fellowship with God, not a spasmodic demand for his gifts. Many people associate prayer exclusively with some special posture, such as kneeling, and with the verbal utterance of their particular wants. They often are disturbed because this act gives them no help, because it issues in no perceptible result at all.

But even a casual acquaintance with the biographies of praying men makes clear that praying is to them a very different thing from saying prayers. One who all her life had identified with prayer certain appointed acts of devotion, properly timed and decently performed, exclaimed "Prayer has entirely left my life"; yet when asked whether she never was conscious of an unseen Presence in fellowship with whom she found peace and strength, she answered, "I could not live without *that!*" Well, that *is* prayer—"not a mechanical repetition of verbal forms," as A. C. Benson puts it, "but a strong and secret uplifting of the heart to the Father of all."

Let any of the spiritual seers describe the innermost meaning of prayer to them, and always this habitual attitude of secret communion lies at the heart of the matter; they are seeking God himself, rather than his outward gifts. As Horace Bushnell says: "I fell into the habit of talking with God on every occasion. I talk myself asleep at night, and open the morning talking with him"; and Jeremy Taylor describes his praying as "making frequent colloquies and short discoursings between God and his own soul"; and Sir Thomas Browne, the famous physician, says, "I have resolved to pray more and to pray always, to pray in all places where quietness inviteth, in the house, on the highway, and on the street; and to know no street or passage in this city that may not witness that I have not forgotten God." Ask a monk like Brother Lawrence what praying means to him; and he answers, "That we should establish ourselves in a sense of God's presence, by continually conversing with Him"; and ask the question of so different a man as Carlyle, and the reply springs from the same idea, "Prayer is the aspiration of our poor, struggling, heavy-laden soul toward its Eternal Father, and with or without words, ought not to become impossible, nor, I persuade myself, need it ever."

To be sure, this habitual attitude is helped, not hindered, by occasional acts of devotion. Patriotism should extend over all the year, but that end is encouraged and not halted by special anniversaries like Independence Day; gratitude should be a continuous attitude, but all the months are thankfuller because of Thanksgiving Day; "Remember the week day to keep it holy" is a great commandment, but the experience of the race is clear that to keep one day each week uniquely sacred makes all days sacreder. So if all hours are to be in some degree God-conscious, some hours should be deliberately so. The biographies of praying men reveal regularity as well as spontaneity. One would expect John Wesley to undertake anything methodically, and prayer is no exception. In addition to his voluminous Journal, Wesley kept diaries, scores of which have been preserved, and on the first page of each this vow is found: "I resolve, *Deo juvante,* (1) to devote an hour morning and evening to private prayer, no pretense, no excuse whatsoever; and (2) to converse κατὰ θεόν (face to face with God), no lightness, no εὐτραπελία (facetiousness)." The greatest praying has generally meant habitual communion with God that expressed itself in occasional acts, and occasional acts that deepened habitual communion; but whatever the method, alike the basis and the end of all was abiding fellowship with God.

> "There is a viewless, cloistered room,
>   As high as heaven, as fair as day,
> Where, though my feet may join the throng,
>   My soul can enter in, and pray.
>
> One hearkening, even, cannot know
>   When I have crossed the threshold o'er;
> For He alone, who hears my prayer,
>   Has heard the shutting of the door."

IV

For another thing, the thought of prayer as communion with God *relieves us from the pressure of many intellectual difficulties.* To pray for detailed gifts from God, to ask him in the realm where the laws of nature reign to serve us in this particular, or to refrain in that— this sort of entreaty raises puzzling questions that baffle thought. To commune with God, however, is not only prayer in its deepest meaning; it is prayer in its simplest, most intelligible form. Here, at least, we can confidently deal with reality in prayer, undisturbed by the problems that often confuse us. For the standard objections to prayer —the reign of natural law making answer impossible, the goodness and wisdom of God making changes in his plans undesirable—need not trouble us here. When a man sits in fellowship with his friend, neither begging for things, nor trying to content himself with soliloquy, but gaining the inspiration, vision, peace, and joy which friendship brings through mutual communion, he does not fear the reign of law. *The law of friendship is communion, and prayer is the fulfilling of the law.* So fellowship in the spirit may be free and unencumbered, theoretical perplexities may be left far behind; and we may range out into a transforming experience of the divine friendship, when we learn that prayer is not beggary, it is not soliloquy, it is communion with God.

This interpretation of the innermost nature of prayer as the search of the soul for God rather than for his gifts, has, to some, a modern sound, as though it were new—invented, perhaps, to put the possibility of praying out of reach of this generation's special difficulties. But to call this view modern is to betray ignorance of what the choicest people of God in all centuries have meant by praying. Recall St. Augustine's entreaty in the fourth century, "Give me thine own self, without whom, though thou shouldst give me all that ever thou hadst made, yet could not my desires be satisfied." Recall Thomas à Kempis in the fifteenth century, praying, "It is too small and unsatisfactory, whatsoever thou bestowest on me, apart from thyself." And then recall George Matheson in the nineteenth century: "Whether thou comest in sunshine or in rain, I would take thee into my heart joyfully. Thou art thyself more than the sunshine; thou art thyself compensation for the rain. It is thee and not thy gifts I crave." This view of prayer is neither peculiarly modern nor ancient; it is the common property of all Christian seers who have penetrated to the heart of praying. The intellectual puzzles are found in the fringes of prayer; prayer at its center is as simple and as profound as friendship.

v

The inevitable effect of this sort of communion is that God becomes real. *Only to one who prays can God make himself vivid.* Robertson of Brighton has already described for us his crude ideas of prayer in his boyhood. Listen to him, however, as at the age of twenty-five he writes: "It seems to me now that I can always see, in uncertainty, the leading of God's hand after prayer, when everything seems to be made clear and plain before the eyes. In two or three instances I have had evidence of this which I cannot for a moment doubt." An experience like this makes God vivid, but to many people God is only a vague Being in whom they dimly believe but with whom they have no dealings. They have heard of him in the home from childhood and never have entirely escaped the influence of their early teaching about him; they have heard of him in the church and find it difficult to doubt what everywhere, always, and by all has been believed concerning him; they have heard of him from the philosophers, and when a scientist like Sir Oliver Lodge says, "Atheism is so absurd that I do not know how to put it into words," they see no reason to dispute. But all this is like the voice of many astronomers saying that there are rings about Saturn. Men believe it who never saw the rings. They believe it, but the rings have no influence upon their lives. They believe it, but they have no personal dealings with the object of their faith. So men think that God is, but they never have *met him.* They never have come into that personal experience of communion with God which says: *"I had heard of thee by the hearing of the ear; but now mine eye seeth thee."* (Job 42:5).

Nothing is real to us except those things with which we habitually deal. Men say that they do not pray because to them God is not real, but a truer statement generally would be that God is not real because they do not pray. *Granted a belief that God is, the practice of prayer is necessary to make God not merely an idea held in the mind but a Presence recognized in the life.* In an exclamation that came from the heart of personal religion, the Psalmist cried, "O God, thou art *my* God" (Psalm 63:1). To stand afar off and say "O God," is neither difficult nor searching. We do it when we give intellectual assent to a creed that calls God "Infinite in being and perfection; almighty, most wise, most holy, most free, most absolute; working all things according to the counsel of his own immutable and most righteous will." In such a way to say, "O God," is easy, but it is an inward and searching matter to say, "O God, thou art *my* God." The first is theology, the second is religion; the first involves only opinion, the second involves vital experience; the first can be reached by thought, the second must be reached by prayer; the first leaves God afar off, the second alone makes him real. To be sure, all Christian service where we consciously ally ourselves with God's purpose, and all insight into history where we see God's providence at work, help to make God real to us; but there is an inward certainty of God that can come only from personal communion with God. *"God,"* said Emerson, *"enters by a private door into every individual."*

One day in Paris, a religious procession carrying a crucifix passed

Voltaire and a friend. Voltaire, who was generally regarded as an infidel, lifted his hat. "What!" the friend exclaimed, "are you reconciled with God?" And Voltaire with fine irony replied: *"We salute, but we do not speak."* That phrase is a true description of many men's relationship with God. They believe that God is; they cannot explain the universe without him; they are theists, but they maintain no personal relationships with him. They salute, but they do not speak. They believe in the church, and, especially in sensitive moments when some experience has subdued them to reverence, they are moved by the dignity and exaltation of the church's services, but they have no personal fellowship with God. They salute, but they do not speak.

When men complain, then, that God is not real to them, the reply is fair: How *can* God be real to some of us? What conditions have we fulfilled that would make anybody real? Those earthly friendships have most vivid reality and deepest meaning for us, where a constant sense of spiritual fellowship is refreshed occasionally by special reunions. The curtain that divides us from the thought of our friend is never altogether closed, but at times soul talks with soul in conscious fellowship. The friend grows real. We enter into new thankfulness for him, new appreciation of him, new intimacy with him. No friendship can sustain the neglect of such communion. Even God grows unreal, ceases to be our Unseen Friend and dwindles into a cold hypothesis to explain the world, when we forget communion.

Jude expressed a deep insight into the necessities of the spiritual life, when he said: *"Keep yourselves in the love of God"* (vs. 21).

SUGGESTIONS FOR THOUGHT AND DISCUSSION

What are the primary practical difficulties in prayer?

Why does a child lose confidence in prayer if it is not literally answered?

How far do men continue to pray who believe in prayer as spiritual exercise?

What difficulties in prayer are set forth in Psalm 22:1-5? How far are these typical?

In your experience, what have been the chief practical difficulties in praying?

If no petition were ever answered, would it still be worth while to pray?

What light does the Bible throw upon these practical difficulties?

What was the difference in the prayer of the prodigal on leaving and returning home?

What was the essential element in prayer in the experience of Jesus? Did Jesus receive everything he prayed for? Why did Jesus pray?

Why did the disciples ask Jesus to teach them to pray?

Why is communion with God the central idea of prayer?

What is the greatest gift that any friend gives another? What is the essence of any personal relationship? Is this true of relationship with God?

How does communion with God differ from the experience of human friendship?

What effect upon the prayer life has the experience of prayer as communion with God?

What is necessary for the maintenance of communion with God?

CHAPTER III

God's Care for the Individual

DAILY READINGS

First Day, Third Week

Perhaps the greatest single difficulty in maintaining the habit of prayer is our tendency to make of it a *pious form* and not a *vital transaction.* We begin by trying to pray and end by saying prayers. To urge ourselves to a practice that has thus become a stereotyped and lifeless form is futile. Nobody ever succeeds in praying as a *tour de force;* but if the act of prayer can be seen as the great Christians have seen it—a vital and sustaining friendship with a God who cares for every one of us—praying will cease being a form and become a force and a privilege. Note the vitality of prayer as the Psalmist has experienced it:

My soul, wait thou in silence for God only;
For my expectation is from him.
He only is my rock and my salvation:
He is my high tower; I shall not be moved.
With God is my salvation and my glory:
The rock of my strength, and my refuge, is in God.
Trust in him at all times, ye people;
Pour out your heart before him:
God is a refuge for us.—Psalm 62:5-8.

In confirmation of this same experience in our own day, consider the testimony of Sir Wilfred Grenfell: "The privilege of prayer to me is one of the most cherished possessions, because faith and experience alike convince me that God himself sees and answers, and his

answers I never venture to criticise. It is only my part to ask. It is
entirely his to give or withhold, as he knows is best. If it were otherwise, I would not dare to pray at all. In the quiet of home, in the
heat of life and strife, in the face of death, the privilege of speech
with God is inestimable. I value it more because it calls for nothing
that the wayfaring man, though a fool, cannot give—that is, the
simplest expression to his simplest desire. When I can neither see,
nor hear, nor speak, still I can pray so that God can hear. When I
finally pass through the valley of the shadow of death, I expect to
pass through it in conversation with him."

*O Lord, renew our spirits and draw our hearts unto Thyself that
our work may not be to us a burden, but a delight; and give us such
a mighty love to Thee as may sweeten all our obedience. Oh, let us
not serve Thee with the spirit of bondage as slaves, but with the
cheerfulness and gladness of children, delighting ourselves in Thee
and rejoicing in Thy work. Amen.*—Benjamin Jenks (1646-1724).

Second Day, Third Week

One of the root reasons why prayer becomes merely a pious form
is that while people believe in God in a general and vague fashion,
*they do not vividly grasp the idea that God cares for and is dealing
with every one of us.*

**How think ye? If any man have a hundred sheep, and one of
them be gone astray, doth he not leave the ninety and nine, and
go unto the mountains, and seek that which goeth astray? And if so
be that he find it, verily I say unto you, he rejoiceth over it more
than over the ninety and nine which have not gone astray. Even
so it is not the will of your Father who is in heaven, that one of
these little ones should perish.—Matt. 18:12-14.**

A man may hold true this individual care of God for each of his
children, and still may not practice habitual prayer, but it is difficult
to see how anyone can practice habitual prayer if he does not hold
for true that God loves every one of us. Who can continue praying,
in any Christian sense, to a God that does not care? *For prayer, at
least, a God who does not care, does not count.* Haeckel, the mate-
rialist, has displaced the Creator by a primal substance which he

solemnly crowns Emperor of the universe under the title of "Mobile Cosmic Ether." Can we imagine anyone finding vital and sustaining help in supplications addressed to such an object, or are vast congregations likely to be stirred in adoration, praying, "O Mobile Cosmic Ether, hallowed be thy name!" Why not? Is not the reason simply this, that the God to whom real prayer is made must care for us as a race and as individuals?

Almighty God, the refuge of all that are distressed, grant unto us that, in all trouble of this our mortal life, we may flee to the knowledge of Thy lovingkindness and tender mercy; that so, sheltering ourselves therein, the storms of life may pass over us, and not shake the peace of God that is within us. Whatsoever this life may bring us, grant that it may never take from us the full faith that Thou art our Father. Grant us Thy light, that we may have life, through Jesus Christ our Lord. Amen.—George Dawson (1821-1876).

Third Day, Third Week

Are not two sparrows sold for a penny? and not one of them shall fall on the ground without your Father: but the very hairs of your head are all numbered. Fear not therefore: ye are of more value than any sparrows.—Matt. 10:29-31.

Let us face again today that formality in prayer that comes from a failure to grasp the individual love of God. There are real difficulties for the mind to face when it tries to believe that God so cares for each of us, but perhaps even greater for most people is the difficulty that the *imagination* faces. In this vast universe how can we picture God as caring for every individual thing, even to stricken sparrows and to the hairs of our head? Consider, however, the scientific truth of gravitation, that the whole earth rises to meet a child's ball, just as truly as the ball falls to meet the earth, and that only the lack of sensitiveness in our instruments prevents us from measuring the earth's ascent as it responds to the pull of the child's toy. Can we imagine that? Is it not unimaginable, though plainly true? And if in a gravitate system a whole planet moves to meet a tossed ball, we ought not to dismiss, for reasons of weak imagination, the truth that in a love-system of persons, the Eternal God responds to each child's approach. As Kipling sings:

> "Who clears the grounding berg,
> And guides the grinding floe,
> He hears the cry of the little kit fox,
> And the lemming on the snow."

O Thou good omnipotent, who so carest for every one of us, as if Thou caredst for him alone; and so for all, as if all were but one! Blessed is the man who loveth Thee, and his friend in Thee, and his enemy for Thee. I behold how some things pass away that others may replace them, but Thou dost never depart. O God, my Father, supremely good, Beauty of all things beautiful, to Thee will I intrust whatsoever I have received from Thee, and so shall I lose nothing. Thou madest me for Thyself, and my heart is restless until it repose in Thee. Amen.—St. Augustine (354-430).

Fourth Day, Third Week

Neither for these only do I pray, but for them also that believe on me through their word; that they may all be one; even as thou, Father, art in me, and I in thee, that they also may be in us: that the world may believe that thou didst send me. And the glory which thou hast given me I have given unto them; that they may be one, even as we are one; I in them, and thou in me, that they may be perfected into one; that the world may know that thou didst send me, and lovedst them, even as thou lovedst me.—John 17:20-23.

It is easy to think that God's love centered about the Master, but consider what it would mean for prayer vitally to believe that God so cares for each of us—*"lovedst them, even as thou lovedst me!"* As Silvester Horne puts it in his Yale lectures: "What is the Gospel? —It is contained in a verse of one of the greatest Christian hymns:

> 'Were the whole realm of Nature mine,
> That were a present far too small!
> Love so amazing, so Divine,
> Demands my soul!——'

That is to say that my soul is a greater and bigger thing than the whole realm of nature. Do you believe it? I agree it is the most romantic of all beliefs. It affirms that the soul of every forced laborer on the Amazon is of more value than all the mines of Johannesburg, all the diamonds of Kimberley, all the millions of all the magnates of

America. It affirms that in God's sight all the suns and stars that people infinite space, are of inferior worth to one human spirit dwelling, it may be, in the degraded body of some victim of drink or lust, some member of the gutter population of a great city who has descended to his doom by means of the multiplied temptations with which our so-called society environs him. It is a romantic creed. But if it is not true Christianity itself is false." *Has your failure in prayer been due to your failure in apprehending for yourself this heart of the Gospel?*

O God, mercifully grant unto us that the fire of Thy love may burn up in us all things that displease Thee, and make us meet for Thy heavenly Kingdom.—Roman Breviary.

Fifth Day, Third Week

For we have not a high priest that cannot be touched with the feeling of our infirmities; but one that hath been in all points tempted like as we are, yet without sin. Let us therefore draw near with boldness unto the throne of grace, that we may receive mercy, and may find grace to help us in time of need.—Hebrews 4:15, 16.

Note the sequence of thought in these verses: first, the revelation in Christ of a God who cares; and second, resultant confidence in the reality of prayer. In contrast with this reality of prayer to those who apprehend the personal love of God, consider how many people know prayer only as an *inherited bit of propriety*. Prayer to them is a formality because it is a practice taught in infancy, and maintained by force of habit as a tradition. It is not vital. It does not mean "Grace to help us in time of need." They are true to George Eliot's description of Hetty in Adam Bede: "Hetty was one of those numerous people who have had god-fathers and god-mothers, learned their catechism, been confirmed, and gone to church every Sunday, and yet for any practical result of strength in life, or trust in death, have never appropriated a single Christian idea or Christian feeling." Over against such a futile form of religion consider a vital prayer like this of Thomas à Kempis, founded on the thought of God's individual love.

Ah, Lord God, Thou holy Lover of my soul, when Thou comest into my soul, all that is within me shall rejoice. Thou art my Glory

*and the exultation of my heart; Thou art my Hope and Refuge in
the day of my trouble. Set me free from all evil passions, and heal
my heart of all inordinate affections; that, being inwardly cured
and thoroughly cleansed, I may be made fit to love, courageous to
suffer, steady to persevere. Nothing is sweeter than Love, nothing
more courageous, nothing fuller nor better in heaven and earth;
because Love is born of God, and cannot rest but in God, above all
created things. Let me love Thee more than myself, nor love myself
but for Thee. Amen.*—Thomas à Kempis (1379-1471).

Sixth Day, Third Week

To many people prayer is a pious practice rather than a vital
transaction, not so much because it is an inherited bit of propriety,
but because it is looked upon as a *good work which wins merit* in the
eyes of God. Men think of prayer as a safe practice to indulge in if
they are to keep on good terms with God. They go through it as a
courtier might observe the rituals of obeisance that please the king
and the neglect of which might get a careless man into trouble.
Prayer to many is a safety appliance, like a lightning-rod, upward
raised lest the Eternal God, seeing their neglect, fall foul of them.
It is founded on fear. They conceive that the saying of prayer is a
measure of protection which they would better attend to. *What a
pitiful misunderstanding of prayer!* Prayer is not a "good work" in
return for which a blessing is given, as men buy and sell over the
counter. Our pious practices are as useless as a Tibetan prayer
wheel, unless at the heart of them all is conscious fellowship with the
Father who cares.

Listen to Isaiah's expression of God's contempt for formal worship
without spiritual meaning:

What unto me is the multitude of your sacrifices? saith Jehovah:
I have had enough of the burnt-offerings of rams, and the fat of fed
beasts; and I delight not in the blood of bullocks, or of lambs, or
of he-goats. When ye come to appear before me, who hath required
this at your hand, to trample my courts? Bring no more vain obla-
tions; incense is an abomination unto me; new moon and sabbath,
the calling of assemblies,—I cannot away with iniquity and the
solemn meeting. Your new moons and your appointed feasts my
soul hateth; they are a trouble unto me; I am weary of bearing

them. And when ye spread forth your hands, I will hide mine eyes from you; yea, when ye make many prayers, I will not hear: your hands are full of blood.—Isaiah 1:11-15.

Most loving Lord, give me a childlike love of Thee, which may cast out all fear. Amen.—E. B. Pusey (1800-1882).

Seventh Day, Third Week

For as many as are led by the Spirit of God, these are sons of God. For ye received not the spirit of bondage again unto fear; but ye received the spirit of adoption, whereby we cry, Abba, Father. The Spirit himself beareth witness with our spirit, that we are children of God: and if children, then heirs; heirs of God, and joint-heirs with Christ.—Romans 8:14-17.

In the light of this passage how impossible to think of saying prayers as merely a pious practice. Prayer seen in the light of this Christian truth becomes at once the *claiming of our sonship, the appropriation of our heritage.* All through the New Testament the reader is conscious that wealth is waiting to be claimed. "Unsearchable riches of Christ," "Rich toward God," "Heirs of God," phrases such as these suggest the sense of spiritual wealth in which the first Christians rejoiced. They had found an Eldorado in the Gospel that God loved every son of man. Now, prayer is the active appropriation of this wealth. Of how many of us is it true that friendship with God is an *unclaimed heritage!* We have the title-deeds in our church membership, but we do not have the spiritual riches in our lives. *In our prayers we are not appropriating our faith that God really does care.*

Grant me, even me, my dearest Lord, to know Thee, and love Thee, and rejoice in Thee. And, if I cannot do these perfectly in this life, let me at least advance to higher degrees every day, till I can come to do them in perfection. Let the knowledge of Thee increase in me here, that it may be full hereafter. Let the love of Thee grow every day more and more here, that it may be perfect hereafter; that my joy may be great in itself, and full in Thee. I know, O God, that Thou art a God of truth; O make good Thy gracious promises to me, that my joy may be full. Amen.—St. Augustine (354-430).

COMMENT FOR THE WEEK

When a man, making earnest with prayer, sets himself to practice communion with God, he is likely to awaken with a start some day to a disturbing reflection. "This thing that I am doing," he well may say, "presupposes that the Almighty God takes a personal interest in me. I am taking for granted when I pray that the Eternal is specially solicitous on my behalf. Praying may seem a simple matter, but on what an enormous assumption does it rest!" Now, this reflection accords entirely with the facts. Prayer does involve confidence that God takes interest in the individual who prays. The fact, for example, that the Bible is preeminently a book of prayer, involves of necessity the companion fact that the God of the Bible cares for individuals. He knows all the stars by name (Psalm 147:4); he numbers the hairs of our heads (Matt. 10:30); of all the sparrows "not one of them is forgotten in the sight of God" (Luke 12:6). John is expressing his thought of God as well as his interpretation of Christ when he says, "He calleth his own sheep by name" (John 10:3). God is like a shepherd who misses even one lost from his flock, a housewife who seeks for a single coin, a father who grieves for one boy gone wrong (Luke 15). Of all the children in the world, says Jesus, "It is not the will of your Father . . . that *one of these* little ones should perish" (Matt. 18:14). Throughout the Bible, and especially in the New Testament, God is not a king dealing with men in masses. He is no Napoleon, who, warned by Metternich that a campaign would cost a million men, said, "What are a million men to me?" God is a father, and the essence of fatherhood is individual care for the children. For all that there are so many of us, as St. Augustine said, *"He loves us every one as though there were but one of us to love."* That is the message of the Book, and it underlies the possibility of vital prayer.

This truth that God cares for every one of us is easy to speak about, beautiful to contemplate, but hard to believe. How *can* God care for each of us? We know the heart of Jesus well enough to understand that he loved every one he met. But *God?* How can we make it real to ourselves that he who sustains the milky way, who holds Orion and the Pleiades in his leash, knows us by name?

II

For one thing, we seem too small and insignificant for him to know. If God cares for each of us, that presupposes in us a degree of value and importance surpassing imagination; and as one considers the vastness of the physical universe, it seems almost unbelievable that individual men can be worth so much. Even the Psalmist felt the wonder of man's worth in such a world, when he cried: "When I consider thy heavens, the work of thy fingers, the moon and the stars, which thou hast ordained; what is man, that thou art mindful of him? And the son of man, that thou visitest him?" (Psalm 8:3, 4). The Psalmist, however, never saw more than 6,000 stars on the clearest night when he looked at the sky from the heights of Zion. We today can see 100,000,000 of them through our telescopes; and when we put a photographic plate, instead of our eyes, at the orifice of the instrument, we obtain indications of multitudes more. When, therefore, a modern psalmist like Tennyson thinks of man's possible value in so great a universe, he feels the terrific urge of doubt; he gathers all the activities of mankind, our wars, politics, arts and sciences, and cries,

"What is it all but a trouble of ants in the gleam of a million million of suns?"

How in the face of this new knowledge of the universe can we pray in the confidence that God knows and cares for each one of us?

Many a man's faith is undone and his prayers stopped by this appalling contrast between the size of the world and his own smallness. The *microscope,* however, should counteract a little the disheartening influence of the *telescope.* It is evident that the Power which cares for the stars cares for all things with utter disregard of size. Inside any common pin as marvelous activity is going on as ever was present among the stars. Here are electrons so many and so small that the race in a million years could not count them, and yet not one electron touches another. In comparison with their size they are as far apart as the planets of a solar system. Endlessly they revolve about each other, and no one ever slips by an infinitesimal degree from the control of law. Not strong reason but weak imagination leads us to be terrified by the mere size of the universe into the thought that God cannot care for us. So far as physical nature has any testimony to bear on the matter at all, she says, "There is noth-

ing too great for the Creator to accomplish, and nothing too small
for him to attend to. The microscopic world is his, as well as the
stars."

The real answer to our doubt, however, comes not from physical
nature at all, but from spiritual insight. We are so small that God
cannot care for every one of us? *But surely, we ourselves are not
accustomed to judge comparative value by size.* As children we may
have chosen a penny rather than a dime because the penny was
larger; but as maturity arrives, that basis of choice is outgrown. The
dearest possessions of the human race—diamonds and little children,
for example—are rather notable for their comparative smallness. A
mother's love for her baby is not a matter of pounds and ounces.
When one believes in God at all, the consequence is plain. God must
have at least our spiritual insight to perceive the difference between
size and *worth*. Mere bulk cannot deceive him. He must know where
in all his universe the real values lie.

As to where the real values *do* lie, the thoughtful of all races have
unanimously agreed that they are found inside personality, not outside of it. Tennyson's word is a summary of the best thought of all
time:

> "For tho' the Giant Ages heave the hill
> And break the shore, and evermore
> Make and break, and work their will—
> Tho' world on world in myriad myriads roll
> Round us, each with different powers,
> And other forms of life than ours,
> What know we greater than the soul?"

The thinker is of nobler worth than any external thing that he can
think about; the seer is more wonderful than all he sees; and righteousness, friendship, generosity, courage, wisdom, love, functions of
personality, all of them, are, so far as *value* goes, worth more than
infinite galaxies of stars. No star ever knew that it was even being
gazed upon. No star ever felt God's hand upon it, or was moved by
gratitude for its creation, preservation, and all the blessings of this
life. As an astronomer watches the unconscious heavens, does not
God know, as we do, that the man, with his powers of vision, intellect, volition, and character, is far more marvelous than all the stars
he sees? We may as well deny God's existence altogether, as, granting
his existence, affirm that he is enamoured by hugeness, in love with

avoirdupois, and blind to spiritual values. To gain the whole world
and lose a soul would be a poor bargain for God as well as for man.
Personality is the one infinitely valuable treasure in the universe. If
God is, he cares; if he cares, he cares for personality. "For Jehovah's
portion is his people" (Deut. 32:9).

III

The difficulty which many experience in trying to conceive of
God's individual care, is complicated by the fact that not only are we
small, but *there are countless multitudes of us.* With so many people,
how can God know us all by name? This difficulty is one of the
commonest stumbling blocks to prayer, and yet its mere statement
ought to be its sufficient refutation. Could anything be more plainly
an attempt to make God in man's image than this suggestion that
his powers may be inadequate to his responsibilities? "It is hard for
us to keep individual interest in many people," we are saying, "therefore it must be hard for God." This crude and childish imposition of
our human limitations on God, this fear that he will find it trying
to remember so many, springs not from good reason but from immature thoughtlessness.

> "There was an old woman, who lived in a shoe;
> She had so many children, she didn't know what to do."

Is that nursery rhyme to represent our picture of God?

We may help ourselves to the conception of God's individual care,
which is essential to all vital and earnest praying, by noting that
knowledge, when it moves out toward omniscience, always breaks up
vague masses into individual units, and cares for each of them.
When an ignoramus goes into a library, he can see only long rows
of books, almost indistinguishable as units. But when the librarian
comes, the student and lover of books, he knows each one by name.
Each volume has its special associations; he knows the edition, the
value, the contents, the author, the purpose. He takes down one book
after another, revealing his individual appreciation of each. *The
more he knows, as a librarian, the less he sees books in the mass; the
more he knows them one by one.*

Increasing knowledge is always thus not *extensive* only but *inten-
sive.* The average man returns from seeing the turbines at Niagara,
with a vague impression of enormous masses moving at tremendous

speed. But the engineer? He knows every bolt and screw, every lever and piston; he knows the particular details of secret bearing and balanced strain; he pokes his wrench around dark corners for hidden bolts that the spectator never guessed were there. The more he knows, as an engineer, the more he sees the details and not the bulk. *Ignorance sees things in mass; knowledge breaks all masses up into units and knows each one; omniscience perfectly understands and cares for every most minute detail.*

Consider then the meaning of God's knowledge of men. When a stranger thinks of China he imagines a vague multitude, with faces that look all alike. When a missionary thinks of China, the vague multitude is shaken loose in one spot, and individuals there stand out, separately known and loved. When God thinks of China, he knows every one of the Chinese by name. He does for humanity what a librarian does for his books, or an engineer for his turbines. We stand, every one, separate in his thought. He lifts us up from the obscurity of our littleness; he picks us out from the multitude of our fellows; he gives to our lives the dignity of his individual care. The Eternal God calls us every one by name. He is not the God of mankind in the mass; he is the God of *Abraham,* of *Isaac,* and of *Jacob!* All great pray-ers have lived in the power of this individual relationship with God. They have said with the Psalmist,

> "*I* will give thanks in the *great assembly:*
> *I* will praise thee among *much people.*"
> (Psalm 35:18.)

IV

So important is the vital apprehension of this truth that we may well approach it from another angle. When one believes in God at all, he must believe that God has a purpose for the universe as a whole. The seers have uttered this faith in scores of figures, but no one of them is adequate to express the full meaning of this confidence that creation means something, has a goal, is not a blind accident, but a wise plan. "Nothing walks with aimless feet," says Tennyson. "There are no accidents with God," says Longfellow. All who believe in God must somehow share this faith. For them there is a divine purpose that "binds in one book the scattered leaves of all the universe." Indeed, most men *do* believe this. The contrary position makes life too empty and futile to be easily tolerable. If there is

no purpose in creation at all, if it came from nowhere, is going nowhere, and means nothing, then the world is like a busy seamstress
sewing on a machine with no thread in it. The centuries move like
cloths beneath the biting needle, but no thread binds them. Nothing
is being done. The years will pass; the machine will wear out; the
scrap-heap will claim it; but there will be nothing to show for all its
toil. That is the world without divine purpose; and because such an
outlook on life makes it utterly vain and futile, most men do believe
in "one far-off divine event, toward which the whole creation
moves." They believe that there is a thread of divine purpose in this
machine of the universe and that it binds the separate centuries
together.

As soon as we speak of this general purpose of God, however, an
inevitable corollary faces us. *Can God have a purpose for the whole
and not for the parts?* Can an architect thoroughly plan a house
without planning the details? Shall he stand upon the site and say in
a vague and sweeping way, "Let there be a house"? But, if you ask
him about the chimney angles and the window frames, shall he
answer, "There is no plan for them"? Rather planning a house consists in arranging the parts. And when we turn from dealing with
things to deal with persons, each one so individual and unique, how
much more clear the truth is! *No father can love his family in general, without loving the several members of it in particular.* So God
can neither care nor plan for his world as a whole, without caring
and planning for each of the individuals that make his world. The
faith of the Bible, in the individual knowledge, love, and purpose of
God for each of us is not mere sentiment. It is the inevitable corollary of theism. No man can think through the meaning of belief in
God without coming to it. Purpose for the universe and purpose for
each life are two aspects of the same thing and they mutually involve
each other. You can as easily find a shield with only one side as a
purpose that concerns the whole and not the parts. Here, too, God
calls us every one by name. As an Indian poet sings,

"The subtle anklets that ring on the feet of an insect when it moves
    are heard of Him."

Whether, therefore, we consider the fact that God must care for
value rather than for size; or the fact that knowledge, as it grows,
always breaks up masses into units and understands each one of

them; or the fact that no love and purpose in general can fail to include the particular parts, we come to the same conclusion: God's individual care for us is not only a reasonable, it is an inevitable corollary of our faith. Of course, God numbers the hairs of our heads! Just that sort of thing infinite knowledge necessarily implies. Of course, the Scripture cries in a passage, quoted by Jesus, "All of you sons of the Most High!" (Psalm 82:6). Just that *must* be said when the fatherhood of God is believed at all. Of course, it is not God's will that "one of these little ones should perish" (Matt. 18:14). How could he care for all and not for each? Of course, Jesus says, "Having shut thy door, pray to thy Father who is in secret" (Matt. 6:6). For trust in God's individual love, if it have normal growth, must always flower out in prayer.

v

Indeed, prayer is the personal appropriation of this faith that God cares for each of us. When a man really prays he no longer leaves his thought of God's individual care as a theory, held in his mind, beautiful but ineffective. He now avails himself of the truth which he sees; he thrusts his life out upon it; he enters into that fellowship with God of which the creed is the theory, and prayer is the practice. It is one thing to think that a man is your friend; it is another thing actively to enter into friendly relations with him. So some men merely believe that God is, and that he cares for them; but some richly profit by their faith, so acting upon it in prayer that vague belief about God passes over into transforming relationship with him. Belief by itself is a map of the unvisited land of God's care; prayer is actually traveling the country. The tragedy of the Church is to be found in the thousands who fondle their credal maps, on which are marked the roadways of God's friendship, but who do not travel. They would resent any sceptical doubt about God's love for every individual, but they do not in habitual reliance and communion take advantage of the faith they hold. They miss the daily guidance, the consciousness of divine resource, the sustaining sense of God's presence, which can come only to those who both believe that God cares for each, and who in habitual communion with him are making earnest with their faith.

When, therefore, we have satisfied our minds of God's individual care, we have arrived at the beginning, not at the end of the matter.

Now comes the vital and searching task of laying hold on the *experience* of that care, in whose existence we believe. We must pass from thought into spiritual activity, from the "industrious squirrel work of the brain" into an adventure of the soul in the practice of prayer. The Gospel offers a great privilege; prayer appropriates it. In Calvin's vivid figure, "Prayer *digs out* those treasures which the Gospel of the Lord discovers to our faith."

SUGGESTIONS FOR THOUGHT AND DISCUSSION

What makes prayer a pious form rather than a vital transaction?

What gave vitality to the Psalmist's prayer?

What is the difference between a Buddhist turning a prayer wheel and a Christian praying?

What merit is there in praying?

What is the estimate of the value of the individual in the Christian religion?

What was Jesus' view as set forth in the Daily Readings?

What place has the individual had in the history of the Church?

How does the Christian religion differ from other religions in its estimate of the worth of the individual?

How far are Christians justified in basing their confidence in prayer on God's care for the individual?

Is the possibility of prayer dependent upon God's care for the individual?

To what extent is prayer futile if God does not care for us?

What are your chief difficulties in a belief that God cares for each individual? To what extent do you feel these difficulties make prayer impossible?

How far is it reasonable to think that God cares for us?

What difference will it make in my prayers if I really believe God cares for me as an individual?

CHAPTER IV

Prayer and the Goodness of God

DAILY READINGS

First Day, Fourth Week

And there came near unto him James and John, the sons of Zebedee, saying unto him, Teacher, we would that thou shouldest do for us whatsoever we shall ask of thee. And he said unto them, What would ye that I should do for you? And they said unto him, Grant unto us that we may sit, one on thy right hand, and one on thy left hand, in thy glory. But Jesus said unto them, Ye know not what ye ask. Are ye able to drink the cup that I drink? or to be baptized with the baptism that I am baptized with?—Mark 10:35-38.

Of all misconceptions of prayer, none is more common than the idea that it is a way of *getting God to do our will*. Note the request which James and John made of our Lord: they wanted him to put himself at their disposal; they wished their will for themselves to be in absolute control, with the Master as aider and abettor of it. Prayer to God, so conceived, is simply self-will, expecting the Almighty to back it up and give it right-of-way. Consider how often our praying is thus our demand on God that he shall do exactly what we want; and then in contrast, note this *real* prayer of D. L. Moody:

Use me then, my Saviour, for whatever purpose, and in whatever way, Thou mayest require. Here is my poor heart, an empty vessel; fill it with Thy grace. Here is my sinful and troubled soul; quicken it and refresh it with Thy love. Take my heart for Thine abode; my mouth to spread abroad the glory of Thy name; my love and all my powers, for the advancement of Thy believing people; and never suffer the steadfastness and confidence of my faith to abate—that so at all times I may be enabled from the heart to say, "Jesus needs me, and I Him."—D. L. Moody.

Second Day, Fourth Week

The trouble with many folk is that they *believe in only a part of God*. They believe in his *love*, and thinking of that alone they are led into entreating him as though he might be coaxed and wheedled into giving them what they want. They argue that because he is benign and kindly he will give in to a child's entreaty and do what the child happens to desire. They do not really believe in God's *wisdom*—his knowledge of what is best for all of us, and in his *will*— his plan for the character and the career of each of us. When anyone believes in the whole of God, is sure that he has a wise and a good purpose for every child of his, and for all the world, prayer inevitably becomes not the endeavor to get God to do our will, but the endeavor to open our lives to God so that *God can do in us what he wants to do.* Consider, in the light of this truth, the prayer of the Master in Gethsemane:

Then cometh Jesus with them unto a place called Gethsemane, and saith unto his disciples, Sit ye here, while I go yonder and pray. And he took with him Peter and the two sons of Zebedee, and began to be sorrowful and sore troubled. Then saith he unto them, My soul is exceeding sorrowful, even unto death: abide ye here, and watch with me. And he went forward a little, and fell on his face, and prayed, saying, My Father, if it be possible, let this cup pass away from me: nevertheless, not as I will, but as thou wilt. And he cometh unto the disciples, and findeth them sleeping, and saith unto Peter, What, could ye not watch with me one hour? Watch and pray, that ye enter not into temptation: the spirit indeed is willing, but the flesh is weak. Again a second time he went away, and prayed, saying, My Father, if this cannot pass away, except I drink it, thy will be done. And he came again and found them sleeping, for their eyes were heavy. And he left them again, and went away, and prayed a third time, saying again the same words.—Matt. 26:36-44.

O Lord, Thou knowest what is best for us, let this or that be done, as Thou shalt please. Give what Thou wilt, and how much Thou wilt, and when Thou wilt. Deal with me as Thou thinkest good, and as best pleaseth Thee. Set me where Thou wilt, and deal with me in all things just as Thou wilt. Behold, I am Thy servant, prepared for all things; for I desire not to live unto myself, but unto Thee; and Oh, that I could do it worthily and perfectly! Amen.—Thomas à Kempis (1379-1471).

Third Day, Fourth Week

Let us this week consider particularly the ways in which the practice of prayer opens our lives to God so that his will can be done in and through us. For one thing, prayer, as we now are thinking of it, involves *solitude,* where the voice of God has a chance to be heard.

And when ye pray, ye shall not be as the hypocrites: for they love to stand and pray in the synagogues and in the corners of the streets, that they may be seen of men. Verily I say unto you, They have received their reward. But thou, when thou prayest, enter into thine inner chamber, and having shut thy door, pray to thy Father who is in secret, and thy Father who seeth in secret shall recompense thee.—Matt. 6:5, 6.

Consider the testimony of different sorts of men to the value of occasional solitude in the midst of a busy life. Says Walter Savage Landor, the poet, "Solitude is the ante-chamber of God; only one step more, and you can be in his immediate presence. Goethe says, "No one can produce anything important unless he isolates himself." "Chinese" Gordon writes to his sister, "Getting quiet does one good —it is impossible to hear God's voice in a whirl of visits—you must be more or less in the 'desert' to use the scales of the sanctuary, to see and weigh the true value of things and sayings." And an anonymous epigram hits off the important truth, "He is a wonderful man who can thread a needle while at cudgels in a crowd." *How much time, away from the distractions of business, and the strife of tongues, are we giving to the enriching use of solitude?*

O God, by whom the meek are guided in judgment, and light riseth up in darkness for the godly; grant us, in all our doubts and

*uncertainties, the grace to ask what Thou wouldest have us to do;
that the spirit of Wisdom may save us from all false choices, and
that in Thy light we may see light, and in Thy straight path may not
stumble, through Jesus Christ our Lord. Amen.*—William Bright.

Fourth Day, Fourth Week

Prayer opens our lives to the guidance of God because by its very
nature *it encourages the receptive mood.* The dominant mood today
is active; but some things never come into life until a man is receptive. That a boy should run many errands for his father and should
be faithful and energetic in doing it is of great importance; but the
most far-reaching consequences in that boy's life are likely to come
from some quiet hour, when he sits with his father, and has his eyes
opened to a new *idea of life,* which the father never could give him
in his more active moods. God's trouble to get people to listen is set
forth in the eighty-first Psalm:

Hear, O my people, and I will testify unto thee:
But my people hearkened not to my voice;
And Israel would none of me.
So I let them go after the stubbornness of their heart,
That they might walk in their own counsels.
Oh that my people would hearken unto me.
—Psalm 81:8, 11-13.

*Lord, I know not what I ought to ask of Thee; Thou only knowest
what I need; Thou lovest me better than I know how to love myself.
O Father! give to Thy child that which he himself knows not how
to ask. I dare not ask either for crosses or consolations: I simply
present myself before Thee, I open my heart to Thee. Behold my
needs which I know not myself; see and do according to Thy tender
mercy. Smite, or heal; depress me, or raise me up: I adore all Thy
purposes without knowing them; I am silent; I offer myself in sacrifice: I yield myself to Thee; I would have no other desire than to
accomplish Thy will. Teach me to pray. Pray Thyself in me. Amen.*
—Francois de la Mothe Fénelon (1651-1715).

Fifth Day, Fourth Week

Jesus therefore answered them, and said, My teaching is not
mine, but his that sent me. If any man willeth to do his will, he shall

know of the teaching, whether it is of God, or whether I speak from myself. He that speaketh from himself seeketh his own glory: but he that seeketh the glory of him that sent me, the same is true, and no unrighteousness is in him.—John 7:16-18.

Prayer opens our lives to God so that his will can be done in and through us, because in true prayer we habitually put ourselves into the attitude of *willingness to do whatever God wills*. If a young man says, "I am willing to be a lawyer, but not a business man; I am willing to be a physician, but not a medical missionary," he will never discover what God really wants him to be. He must hand God a *carte blanche* to be filled in as God wills, and there must be no provisos and reservations to limit the guidance of God. If a man of whose wisdom and motives we are suspicious asks us to do what he is about to demand, we may well say, "Tell me what you expect and I will tell you whether or not I will do it." But we may not take that attitude toward God; we may not distrust his wisdom, or his love, or his power to see us through what he demands. We must be willing to do whatever he wills. True prayer is deliberately putting ourselves at God's disposal.

O Lord, let me not henceforth desire health or life, except to spend them for Thee, with Thee, and in Thee. Thou alone knowest what is good for me; do, therefore, what seemeth Thee best. Give to me, or take from me; conform my will to Thine; and grant that, with humble and perfect submission, and in holy confidence, I may receive the orders of Thine eternal Providence; and may equally adore all that comes to me from Thee; through Jesus Christ our Lord. Amen.—Blaise Pascal (1623-1662).

Sixth Day, Fourth Week

And Jehovah spake unto Moses face to face, as a man speaketh unto his friend.—Exodus 33:11.

And the scripture was fulfilled which saith, And Abraham believed God, and it was reckoned unto him for righteousness; and he was called the friend of God.—James 2:23.

The most transforming influences in life are *personal friendships*. Everyone who meets us influences us, but friendship opens the heart to the ideas, ideals, and spiritual quality of another life, until we are susceptible to everything that the friend is and sensitive to everything that he thinks. Desdemona describes the natural effect of close friendship:

> "My heart's subdued
> Even to the very quality of my lord."

Consider then what persistent fellowship with God will mean in changing life's quality and tone. Henry Drummond said, "Ten minutes spent in Christ's society every day; aye, two minutes, if it be face to face and heart to heart, will make the whole life different." In how many people is the fine quality which all feel and none can describe, the result of this inner fellowship! Some things cannot be bought or earned or achieved; they must be *caught*, they are transmitted by contact as fragrance is. Perhaps the greatest consequence of prayer is just this atmosphere which the life carries away with it, as Moses came with shining face from the communion of his heart with God. *True prayer is habitually putting oneself under God's influence.*

We rejoice that in all time men have found a refuge in Thee, and that prayer is the voice of love, the voice of pleading, and the voice of thanksgiving. Our souls overflow toward Thee like a cup when full; nor can we forbear; nor shall we search to see if our prayers have been registered, or whether of the things asked we have received much, or more, or anything. That we have had permission to feel ourselves in Thy presence, to take upon ourselves something of the light of Thy countenance, to have a consciousness that Thy thoughts are upon us, to experience the inspiration of the Holy Spirit in any measure—this is an answer to prayer transcending all things that we can think of. We are glad that we can glorify Thee, that we can rejoice Thee, that it does make a difference to Thee what we do, and that Thou dost enfold us in a consciousness of Thy sympathy with us, of how much Thou art to us, and of what we are to Thee.
—Henry Ward Beecher.

Seventh Day, Fourth Week

Yet thou hast not called upon me, O Jacob; but thou hast been weary of me, O Israel.—Isaiah 43:22.

And there is none that calleth upon thy name, that stirreth up himself to take hold of thee; for thou hast hid thy face from us, and hast consumed us by means of our iniquities.—Isaiah 64:7.

Consider the reasonableness of the prophet's vehement condemnation of prayerlessness, in view of this week's truth. Take out of life solitude where God's voice can be heard, the receptive mood that welcomes guidance, the willingness to do whatever God wills that puts itself habitually at God's disposal, and the fellowship that gives God's secret influence its opportunity; and what can God do with any life? Two very young girls were discussing prayer. Said one: "I am not going to pray again for two weeks." After an interval of shocked silence, the other exclaimed: "Poor God!" Does not this exclamation reveal a true philosophy of prayer? *Think of the things God wants to give to and do through our lives, and consider how the prayerless, unreceptive heart blockades his will.*

Almighty God, and most merciful Father, give us, we beseech Thee, that grace that we may duly examine the inmost of our hearts, and our most secret thoughts, how we stand before Thee; and that we may henceforward never be drawn to do anything that may dishonor Thy name: but may persevere in all good purposes, and in Thy Holy service, unto our life's end; and grant that we may now this present day, seeing it is as good as nothing that we have done hitherto, perfectly begin to walk before Thee, as becometh those that are called to an inheritance of light in Christ. Amen.—George Hickes (1642-1715).

COMMENT FOR THE WEEK

I

Strangely enough, when we have convinced ourselves of the individual love and care of God, we do not so much evade difficulty as encounter it; for we find ourselves running straight into the arms of one of the commonest perplexities concerning prayer. God is all wise and all good; why should we urge on him our erring and ignorant desires? He knows what we need; why tell him? His love purposes the best for us; why beseech him? Why should we, weak and fallible mortals, urge the good God to work good in the world? Is not

Rousseau speaking sound sense when he says: "I bless God, but I pray not. Why should I ask of him that he would change for me the course of things?—I who ought to love, above all, the order established by his wisdom and maintained by his Providence, shall I wish that order to be dissolved on my account?"

This objection to prayer is the stronger because reverence and humility before God seem to be involved in it. "We will take whatever God sends," says the objector, "we will pray for nothing. We trust him perfectly. Can we in our ignorance suggest to him any excellent thing of which he has not thought or which he has forgotten, or can we in our weakness cajole him to do something which he has purposed otherwise? Rather 'Let him do what seemeth him good!' " This sort of speech has the ring of sincere faith. It comes from a strong and glad belief in the providence of God. *The man shrinks from prayer because it seems silly and presumptuous for ignorance to instruct perfect wisdom, for human evil to attempt the persuasion of perfect love to do good.*

It is interesting, then, to discover that the Master's life of urgent prayer was founded on these very ideas which now are used as arguments against prayer. No one, before or since, has believed quite so strongly as he did in the wisdom and love of God. Did they seem to him, then, reasons for abandoning prayer? *On the contrary, the love and wisdom of God were the foundations of his prayer.* In God's goodness he saw a solid reason for praying: "If ye then, being evil, know how to give good gifts unto your children, how much more shall your Father . . . give good things to them that ask him?" (Matt. 7:11). In God's wisdom he found assuring confidence, when he prayed. "Your Father knoweth what things ye have need of, before ye ask him" (Matt. 6:8). Just *because* of God's perfect knowledge and love, the Master seems to say, pray with confidence. Do not think that you can add to God's information about your need or can inspire in him an increased good-will by your petition. You cannot. He knows your need in advance and is more willing to give than you are to take. But one thing you can do. You can open the way for God to do what he wants to do. Prayer cannot change God's purpose, but prayer can release it. God cannot do for the man with the closed heart what he can do for the man with the open heart. You can give God a chance to work his will in and for and through you. *Prayer is simply giving the wise and good God an opportunity to do what his wisdom and love want done.*

II

This point of view is the distinguishing element in the Christian conception of prayer, and to understand it, is of the utmost importance.

The argument that because God is infinitely good and wise, prayer is a superfluity, rests on two fallacies. The first is the idea that praying is an attempt to secure from God by begging, something which God had not at all intended, or had intended otherwise. But Christian prayer is never that. The African savage beats his fetish when a petition is unanswered. He endeavors to make his god his slave. His one idea is to get what he wants. Christian prayer is giving God an opportunity to do what *he* wants, what he has been trying in vain, perhaps for years, to do in our lives, hindered by our unreadiness, our lack of receptivity, our closed hearts and unresponsive minds. God stands over many lives, like the Master over Jerusalem, saying, "How oft would I . . . and *ye* would not" (Matt. 23:37). True prayer changes that. It opens the door to the will of God. It does not change God's plan, but it does give God's plan gang-way. It is not begging from God; it is cooperation with God. In the luminous words of Archbishop Trench: *"We must not conceive of prayer as an overcoming of God's reluctance, but as a laying hold of his highest willingness."*

The other fallacy underlying the thought that the wisdom and love of God make praying superfluous is the idea that God can do all he wills without any help from us. But he cannot. *The experience of the race is clear that some things God never can do until he finds a man who prays.* Indeed, Meister Eckhart, the mystic, puts the truth with extreme boldness: "God can as little do without us, as we without him." If at first this seems a wild statement, we may well consider in how many ways God's will depends on man's cooperation. God himself cannot do some things unless men *think*. He never blazons his truth on the sky that men may find it without seeking. Only when men gird the loins of their minds and undiscourageably give themselves to intellectual toil, will God reveal to them the truth, even about the physical world. And God himself cannot do some things unless men *work*. Will a man say that when God wants bridges and tunnels, wants the lightnings harnessed and cathedrals built, he will do the work himself? That is an absurd and idle fatalism. God stores the hills with marble, but he never built a Parthenon; he fills the mountains with ore, but he never made a needle or a locomotive. Only when *men* work can some things be done. Recall the words of Stradivarius, maker of violins, as George Eliot interprets him:

> "When any master holds
> 'Twixt chin and hand a violin of mine,
> He will be glad that Stradivari lived,
> Made violins, and made them of the best
> . . . For while God gives them skill
> I give them instruments to play upon,
> God choosing me to help Him.
> . . . If my hand slacked
> I should rob God—since He is fullest good—
> Leaving a blank instead of violins.
> . . . He could not make
> Antonio Stradivari's violins
> Without Antonio."

Now if God has left some things contingent on man's *thinking* and *working* why may he not have left some things contingent on man's *praying?* The testimony of the great souls is a clear affirmative to this: some things never without thinking; some things never without working; some things never without praying! *Prayer is one of the three forms of man's cooperation with God.*

The fact, therefore, that God is all-wise and all-good, is no more reason for abandoning prayer than for abandoning thought and work. At their best, none of them is an endeavor to get anything against the will of God, and all of them alike are necessary to make the will of God dominant in human life. Who would dream of saying, God is all wise, he knows best; he is all good and will give the best; why, therefore, should I either think or work? But that is just as sensible as to say, If God is good, why should I pray? *We pray for the same reason that we work and think, because only so can the wise and good God get some things done which he wants done.*

Indeed, there is a deal of nonsense talked about resignation to God's will as the *only* attitude in prayer. Not resignation to God's will, but cooperation with God's will is the truer expression of a Christian attitude. *We are not resigned anywhere else.* We find an arid desert and, so far from being resigned, we irrigate it until it blossoms like a garden. We find a thorny cactus, and commission Luther Burbank as speedily as possible to make of it a thornless plant for food. We find social evils like slavery, and from Moses to Lincoln all that are best among us are willing to surrender life rather than rest content with wrong. Resignation in the presence of things evil or imperfect is sin; and all the heroes of the race have been so far discontented and unresigned that Blake's challenge has been kindred to their resolution,

> "I will not cease from mental fight,
>   Nor shall my sword sleep in my hand,
>   Till we have built Jerusalem
>   In England's green and pleasant land."

This unresigned attitude, inseparable from nobility of character, is not rebellion against God but cooperation with God. Men act on the assumption that the present situation may be temporarily God's will, but that he has put them in it so that they may fight their way out to a situation that is ultimately his will. To this end they *think* and *work* and *pray.* Resignation is in all three only in the sense that by all three men are endeavoring to open doors for the free passage of God's hindered will. They do not *submit* to God's purpose; they *assert* it. Prayer, like the other two, when it is at its best, never says, Thy will be *changed,* but it says tremendously, Thy will be *done!*

III

That we may clearly perceive God's inability to accomplish his will until men cooperate in prayer, we may note, for one thing, that unless men pray there are some things which God cannot *say* to them. One of our strongest misconceptions concerning prayer is that it consists chiefly in our *talking* to God, whereas the best part of prayer is our *listening* to God. Sometimes in the Scripture a prayer of urgent and definite petition rises, "Oh that I might have my request; And that God would grant me the thing that I long for!" (Job 6:8); but another sort of prayer is very frequently indicated: "Speak; for thy servant heareth" (I Sam. 3:10); "My soul, wait thou in silence for God only; For my expectation is from him" (Psalm 62:5); "I will hear what God Jehovah will speak" (Psalm 85:8); or in Luther's version of Psalm 37:7, "Be silent to God and

let him mold thee." Without such openheartedness to God, some
things which he wills never can be done.

Madame de Staël, after a two hours' visit in which she had talked
continuously, is said to have remarked at parting, "What a delightful
conversation we have had!" Too many prayers are conducted on
that plan. The ironical remark of Savonarola that the saints of his
day were "so busy talking to God that they could not hearken to
him," is applicable to us at least to this extent: *we seldom listen.* We
hammer so busily that the architect cannot discuss the plans with us.
We are so preoccupied with the activities of sailing, that we do not
take our bearings from the sky. When the Spirit stands at the door
and knocks, the bustle of the household tasks drowns the sound of
his knocking. God has a hard time even to get in a word edgewise;
and in lives so conducted, there are some things which God himself,
with all his wisdom and good-will, cannot do. Even a casual study
of the effective servants of the world reveals how much of their
vision and stimulus came in quiet and receptive hours. Prayer gave
God his opportunity to speak, for prayer is the listening ear.

IV

The dependence of God's will upon the cooperation of men's
prayer may be further seen in the fact that until men pray there are
some things which God cannot *give* to them. One of the most disconcerting verses in Scripture tells us that God is more willing to
give to us than fathers are to give to their children (Matt. 7:11).
To some this seems mere sentiment, an exaggerated statement, made
in a poetic hour. To others, who have cried in vain for things that
appeared certainly good, it seems mockery. If God is willing to give,
why doesn't he? What hinders him? How can he be willing to give,
when, being omnipotent, he still withholds? Even a superficial observation of human life, however, could supply the answer. *Giving
is not a simple matter. It is always a dual transaction in which the
recipient is as important a factor as the giver.*

No suffering on earth is more tragic than great love hindered in
its desire to bestow. If a father wishes to give his son an education,
why doesn't he? If he sees the need, has the means, is willing, even
anxious to bestow, what hinders him? In how many cases is the
answer clear: the boy has no genuine desire, no earnest prayer for
the blessing which the father would give. The father is helpless. He

must wait, his love pent, his willingness checkmated, until a prayer, however faint, rises in the boy's heart. The finest gifts cannot be dropped into another's life like stones in a basket. They must be *taken* or else they cannot be *given*. Jesus was thinking of the two factors involved when he said to the Samaritan woman, "If thou knewest the *gift of* God, . . . thou wouldest have *asked*" (John 4:10). The receptive heart is the absolute pre-requisite of all great gifts, and God himself cannot bestow his best on men unless they pray.

Whenever, therefore, we pray intent chiefly on what *we* want, we are likely to be disappointed. But when we pray, intent chiefly on what God wants to give us—perhaps fortitude to bear the trouble which we wish to evade, or patience to wait for the blessing which we demand now, or leadership down a road of service from which we are asking release—we need never be disappointed. Men who come to God not to *dictate* but to *receive* have approached prayer from the right angle. They have seen that prayer is giving God an opportunity to bestow what he is more willing to give than we are to welcome. Prayer is the taking hand. As a sixteenth century mystic said, "Prayer is not to ask what we wish of God, but what God wishes of us."

v

The dependence of God on the cooperation of men's prayer may be further seen in the fact that until men pray there are some things which God cannot *do through them.* Many today, in spite of the busyness, wealth, and efficient organization of our Christian work, bemoan the lack of real power. "What is the matter?" says the practical man. "Have we not taken our time, money, talents and given them in many consecrated and unselfish ways to the service of God? Why, with so many working for God, is not more done?" The answer is written plainly in history. The souls who have ushered in new eras of spiritual life have never been content with *working for God.* They have made it their ideal to *let God work through them.* A scientist has figured that the farmer's toil is five per cent of the energy expended in producing a crop of wheat. The other ninety-five per cent is the universe taking advantage of the chance which the farmer gave it. So these greater servants of God have not thought chiefly of what they could do for God, but of what God could do through them if they gave him opportunity. To be pliable in the hands of God was their first aim. Never to be unresponsive to his will for them was their supreme concern. They said, therefore, with Thomas Hooker, *"Prayer is my chief work, and it is by means of it that I carry on the rest."*

No one can walk through the pages of Scripture, or of Christian biography, with these greater servants of the Kingdom without feeling their power. They are God-possessed. Their characteristic quality is found in Jesus: Not my words, my Father's; not my deeds, his; he that believeth on me, believeth not on me but on him that sent me (John 14:24; 9:4; 5:24). The secret of their lives is like the secret of the Nile: they are the channel of unseen resources. The ideal of such living is deeper than working for God. To release the Eternal Purpose through their lives into the world; to be made a vehicle for power which they do not create but can transmit—this is their ideal. They pray because theirs is the sublime ambition of the German mystic, *"I would fain be to the Eternal Goodness what his own hand is to a man."*

Only through men who take this attitude can God do his choicest work. A life that utterly lacks this attitude, wants the elements of power. When, therefore, a man prays, intent chiefly on what *he* wishes done, his prayer is a failure; but when he prays in order that he may release through his life what God wishes done, he has discovered the great secret. Through him, habitually praying, God can do what else would be impossible. He is one of God's open doors into the world.

VI

We have, then, two fundamentally opposed ideas of prayer: one, that by begging we may change the will of God and curry favor or win gifts by coaxing; the other, that prayer is offering God the opportunity to say to us, give to us, and do through us what he wills. Only the second is Christian. At once we see that the second, no less than the first, and in a way far truer, makes prayer not a form but a force. Prayer really does things. *It cannot change God's intention, but it does change God's action.* God had long intended Isaiah to be his prophet. When Isaiah said, "Here am I, send me," he did not alter in the least the divine purpose, but he did release it. God could *do* then what before he could not. God had long intended that

Africa should be evangelized. When Livingstone cried, "O God, help me to paint this dark continent white," he did not alter God's intention, but he did alter God's action. Power broke loose that before had been pent; the cooperation of a man's prayer, backed by his life, opened a way for the divine purpose. There was an invasion of the world by God through Livingstone. No one can set clear limits to this release of divine power which the effectual prayer of a righteous man can accomplish. Pentecost is typical: "When they had prayed, the place was shaken wherein they were gathered together; and they were all filled with the Holy Spirit, and they spake the word of God with boldness" (Acts 4:31).

SUGGESTIONS FOR THOUGHT AND DISCUSSION

If God is all-wise and all-good, what is the use of praying?

Can prayer change God's plans? If not, what is the use of praying?

How far are God's plans dependent upon individuals?

Can God's purpose be stopped by the failure of an individual to cooperate?

If God is in any way dependent upon the cooperation of individuals, is this inconsistent with his sovereign power and wisdom?

What light do the experiences recorded in the Bible throw upon the problem of prayer and the goodness of God?

In what respect did the request of James and John differ from true prayer?

Why did his belief in the goodness of God give Jesus confidence to pray?

What is the difference in emphasis between the prayer recorded in the eighty-first Psalm and Jesus' comment on the prayer of the hypocrites on the street corners?

In his Gethsemane prayer, what was Jesus' attitude to the will of God?

What place has prayer in the life of every man in finding and doing God's will?

CHAPTER V

Hindrances and Difficulties

DAILY READINGS

First Day, Fifth Week

Howbeit what things were gain to me, these have I counted loss for Christ. Yea verily, and I count all things to be loss for the excellency of the knowledge of Christ Jesus my Lord: for whom I suffered the loss of all things, and do count them but refuse, that I may gain Christ, and be found in him.—Phil. 3:7-9.

We have been speaking of the privilege of prayer, the supreme opportunity of friendship with God kept vital by deliberate communion, and we may well stop now to count the cost. Paul is typical of all Christian seers in discovering that the "excellency of the knowledge of Christ Jesus" is not arrived at without counting some things loss. *It does cost to win a life that really can pray.* Vasari says that Raphael used to wear a candle in a pasteboard cap, so that, while he was painting, his shadow would not fall upon his work. Many a man's prayers are spoiled by his own shadow. There are things in his life which must be given up if ever he is truly to pray. He must wear on his forehead the candle of renunciation for his work's sake. Consider the evil attitudes, cherished sins, bad tempers in your life that make praying in any deep and earnest way a difficult undertaking.

O Lord, come quickly and reign on Thy throne, for now oft-times something rises up within me, and tries to take possession of Thy throne; pride, covetousness, uncleanness, and sloth want to be my kings; and then evil-speaking, anger, hatred, and the whole train of vices join with me in warring against myself, and try to reign over me. I resist them, I cry out against them, and say, "I have no other king than Christ." O King of Peace, come and reign in me, for I will have no king but Thee! Amen.—St. Bernard (1091-1153).

Second Day, Fifth Week

In nothing be anxious; but in everything by prayer and supplication with thanksgiving let your requests be made known unto God. And the peace of God, which passeth all understanding, shall guard your hearts and your thoughts in Christ Jesus. Finally, brethren, whatsoever things are true, whatsoever things are honorable, whatsoever things are just, whatsoever things are pure, whatsoever things are lovely, whatsoever things are of good report; if there be any virtue, and if there be any praise, think on these things.—Phil. 4:6-8.

This connection of verses on great praying and right thinking is not accidental. A man cannot habitually indulge in mean, perverse, or abominable thoughts and suddenly come out of them into unimpeded communion with God. An automobile can be shifted from "low" to "high" with a stroke of the hand, but not so a man's mind. Real praying costs *habitual self-discipline in thinking*—the pure in heart see God. Sherwood Eddy says that the great Madras Young Men's Christian Association building was held up for months, after the site was chosen, the plans drawn, and the money provided, because two shanty-owners would not let go their hold on a little ground in the center of the plot. What is the name of that shanty in your mind which is holding up the great building of character and service for which God has the plans and the means ready?

Most Merciful Father, who orderest the wills and affections of men; inspire in the heart of this Thy servant holy wishes and aspirations, that all base imaginings and sinful broodings may be cast out. Spirit of purity and grace, cleanse the thoughts of his heart and bring his whole being into captivity to the law of Christ. So direct and control his mind that he may ever think on whatsoever things are true and pure and lovely. Let no corrupt thought get dominion over him. Enter Thou into the house of his soul. Enlarge and renew it and consecrate it to Thyself, that he may love Thee with all his

mind and serve Thee with all his might. Free him from the fascina-
tions of false pleasures and the allurements of debasing desires. Fill
his eyes with the eternal beauty of goodness, that vice and sin may
appear as they really are, the last shame and despair of life. Keep
him outwardly in his body and inwardly in his soul, and constrain
him to reverential obedience to the laws Thou hast ordained for
both. Sustain him in health of body that he may the better control
the motions of thought, and repel the assaults of passion. We ask it
for Thy Son our Saviour's sake. Amen.—Samuel McComb.

Third Day, Fifth Week

**Be not rash with thy mouth, and let not thy heart be hasty to
utter anything before God; for God is in heaven, and thou upon
earth: therefore let thy words be few.**—Eccl. 5:2.

Successful prayer involves not only the general preparation of
good living and right thinking; it often costs *special preparation.*
The mood may not be right; an irritated or anxious temper may be
in the way; the preoccupation of business may still be straining our
minds so that if we pray, only a small fraction of us is engaged in it—
a dozen different exigencies may make special preparation an absolute necessity for real prayer. Consider with what rash hastiness,
unprepared thoughts, preoccupied minds, and unexamined lives we
often rush into God's presence and out again. Dr. South puts the
matter with brusque directness, "None but the careless and the confident would rush rudely into the presence of a great man; and shall
we in our applications to the great God, take that to be religion
which the common reason of mankind will not allow to be man-
ners?"

Slay utterly, Oh Lord, and cast down the sin which does so easily
beset us; bridle the unholy affection; stay the unlawful thought;
chasten the temper; regulate the spirit; correct the tongue; bend the
will and the worship of our souls to Thee, and so sanctify and
subdue the whole inward man, that setting up Thy throne in our
hearts, to the dethronement of all our idols, and the things of earth
we hold too dear, Thou mayest reign there alone in the fulness of
Thy grace, and the consolations of Thy presence, till the time arrives
when we shall reign with Thee in glory. Amen.—Richard S. Brooke
(1835-1893).

Fourth Day, Fifth Week

O Jehovah, the God of my salvation,
I have cried day and night before thee.
Let my prayer enter into thy presence;
Incline thine ear unto my cry.
For my soul is full of troubles . . .
Unto thee, O Jehovah, have I cried;
And in the morning shall my prayer come before thee.
Jehovah, why castest thou off my soul?
Why hidest thou thy face from me?

—Psalm 88:1-3, 13, 14.

Such an experience as finds voice in this Psalm suggests at once
that at times prayer costs *persistence in the face of difficulties.* The
unreality of God, the difficulty of holding the mind to the act of
prayer, the wayward mood, the disappointment of the spirit at praying which rings hollow and gives no result—all these difficulties men
of prayer have known. Read the diary of Benjamin Jowett, the great
Master of Balliol, "Nothing makes one more conscious of poverty
and shallowness of character than difficulty in praying or attending
to prayer. Any thoughts about self, thoughts of evil, daydreams, love
fancies, easily find an abode in the mind. But the thought of God
and of right and truth will not stay there, except with a very few
persons. I fail to understand my own nature in this particular. There
is nothing which at a distance I seem to desire more than the knowledge of God, the ideal, the universal; and yet for two minutes I
cannot keep my mind upon them. But I read a great work of fiction,
and can hardly take my mind from it. If I had any real love of God,
would not my mind dwell upon him?"

Gracious Father, who givest the hunger of desire, and satisfiest our
hunger with good things; quicken the heart of Thy servant who
mourns because he cannot speak to Thee, nor hear Thee speak to
him. Refresh, we beseech Thee, the dulness and dryness of his inner
life. Grant him perseverance that he may never abandon the effort
to pray, even though it brings for a time no comfort or joy. Enlarge
his soul's desires that he may be drawn unto Thee. Send forth Thy
Spirit into his heart to help his infirmities; to give him freedom of

utterance, and warmth of feeling. Let him muse upon Thy good-
ness; upon the blessings with which Thou hast strewn his path; upon
the mystery of the world, and the shame of sin, and the sadness of
death,—until the fire kindles and the heart melts in prayer and
praise and supplication.

Lord, teach him to pray the prayer that relieves the burdened
spirit, and brings Thy blessing, which maketh rich and addeth no
sorrow. Hear us, for Jesus' sake. Amen.—Samuel McComb.

Fifth Day, Fifth Week

Give ear to my words, O Jehovah,
Consider my meditation.
Hearken unto the voice of my cry, my King, and my God;
For unto thee do I pray.
O Jehovah, in the morning shalt thou hear my voice;
In the morning will I order my prayer unto thee, and will keep
    watch.—Psalm 5:1-3.

Probably most people are so constituted by nature and are so
preoccupied by business that some such arrangement as is suggested
in this Psalm about regularity is essential to a successful life of
prayer. To be sure, Alice Freeman Palmer, first President of Welles-
ley, has this written of her in her husband's story of her life, "God
was her steady companion, so naturally a part of her hourly thought
that she attached little consequence to specific occasions of intercourse. . . . She had no fixed times of prayer." But before any one
presumes on such a record of fine living with God, minus regularity
of prayer, he would better examine his own character with some
scrutiny. *The chances are in most lives that the keeping of the*
"morning watch" will prove to be one of the most salutary agencies
within the control of the will. This will cost, as regularity always
costs, a persistent determination not to surrender to adverse circumstances or wayward moods. But consider what it would mean each
morning to put the life at God's disposal in some such way as
Thomas à Kempis does in this prayer:

Lord, work in my heart a true Faith, a purifying Hope, and an
unfeigned Love towards Thee; give me a full Trust on Thee, Zeal
for Thee, Reverence of all things that relate to Thee; make me fear-

*ful to offend Thee, Thankful for Thy Mercies, Humble under Thy
Corrections, Devout in Thy Service, and sorrowful for my Sins; and
Grant that in all things I may behave myself so, as befits a Creature
to his Creator, a Servant to his Lord: . . . make me Diligent in all
my Duties, watchful against all Temptations, perfectly Pure and
Temperate, and so Moderate in Thy most Lawful Enjoyments, that
they may never become a Snare to me; make me also, O Lord, to be
so affected towards my Neighbour that I never transgress that Royal
Law of Thine, of Loving him as myself; grant me exactly to perform
all parts of Justice; yielding to all whatsoever by any kind of Right
becomes their due, and give me such Mercy and Compassion, that
I may never fail to do all Acts of Charity to all men, whether Friends
or Enemies, according to Thy Command and Example. Amen.*—
Thomas à Kempis (1379-1471).

Sixth Day, Fifth Week

**And after six days Jesus taketh with him Peter, and James, and
John, and bringeth them up into a high mountain apart by themselves: and he was transfigured before them; and his garments became glistening, exceeding white, so as no fuller on earth can
whiten them. And there appeared unto them Elijah with Moses:
and they were talking with Jesus. And Peter answereth and saith to
Jesus, Rabbi, it is good for us to be here: and let us make three
tabernacles; one for thee, and one for Moses, and one for Elijah.**—
Mark 9:2-5.

How natural for Peter to desire to remain in such a glowing experience! But he could not; it was one of those elevated hours, that
cannot be continuous, but that can reveal outlooks which make all
the dusty traveling afterward more meaningful. Once in a while our
moods go up a mountain and have a great experience, returning
cleansed, exhilarated and reassured. We must cherish such hours,
believe in the validity of their witness to God's presence with us, gain
confidence from their testimony to our sonship with him, and keep
the reassuring memory of life's meaning as we saw it then. But we
must not refuse another sort of praying, less ecstatic and glowing,
more quiet and commonplace. We must not cherish false expectations, demanding transfigured hours continually. Gethsemane is
also prayer and many a lesser time when the soul inwardly steadies

itself on God and trusts where it cannot see. *Successful praying costs this sort of patience with commonplace hours.* Said Fénelon: "Do not be discouraged at your faults; bear with yourself in correcting them, as you would with your neighbor. Accustom yourself gradually to carry prayer into all your daily occupations. Speak, move, work in peace, as if you were in prayer."

O God, Thou hast found us, and not we Thee. At times we but dimly discern Thee; the dismal mists of earth obscure Thy glory. Yet in other and more blessed moments, Thou dost rise upon our souls, and we know Thee as the Light of all our seeing, the Life of all that is not dead within us, the Bringer of health and cure, the Revealer of peace and truth. We will not doubt our better moments, for in them Thou dost speak to us. We rejoice that Thou hast created us in Thine image. Thy love has stirred us into being, has endowed us with spiritual substance. In the intellect, whose thoughts wander through eternity; in the conscience that bears witness to Thy eternal righteousness; in the affections that make life sweet, and reach forth to Thee, O Lover of Mankind—in these, we are made heirs to the riches of Thy grace.—Samuel McComb.

Seventh Day, Fifth Week

Hold not thy peace, O God of my praise;
For the mouth of the wicked and the mouth of deceit have they
    opened against me:
They have spoken unto me with a lying tongue.
They have compassed me about also with words of hatred
And fought against me without a cause.
For my love they are my adversaries:
But I give myself unto prayer.—Psalm 109:1-4.

Such things as these true prayer is likely to cost: a good life, right thinking, special preparations of the mind, persistence through difficulties, regularity, and patience with commonplace hours. But a life that has learned the secret of real praying is worth all that it costs. As the Psalmist says, it is *worth giving ourselves to.* Consider Luther's great description of such a life: "Therefore, where there is a Christian, there is also the Holy Spirit, and he does nothing else save pray continually. For even if the mouth be not always moving and uttering words, yet the heart goes on beating unceasingly with cries like these, Ah! dear Father, may thy name be hallowed, may thy Kingdom come, and thy will be done. And whenever there come sorer buffetings and trials and needs, then the aspiration and supplication increase, even audibly, so that you cannot find a Christian man who does not pray; just as you cannot find a living man without a pulse that never stands still, but beats and beats on continually of itself, although the man may sleep or do anything else, so being all unconscious of this pulse."

Let us today make Archbishop Trench's sonnet our prayer

"If we with earnest effort could succeed
　To make our life one long connected prayer,
　As lives of some perhaps have been and are;
If, never leaving thee, we had no need
Our wandering spirits back again to lead
　Into thy presence, but continue there,
　Like angels standing on the highest stair
Of the sapphire throne,—this were to pray indeed.

But if distractions manifold prevail,
And if in this we must confess we fail,
Grant us to keep at least a prompt desire,
　Continual readiness for prayer and praise,
An altar heaped and waiting to take fire
　With the least spark, and leap into a blaze."

COMMENT FOR THE WEEK

I

A critic with discriminating insight has objected to Voltaire's writings on the ground that nothing could possibly be quite so clear as Voltaire makes it. A book on prayer readily runs into danger of the same criticism. For, like every other vital experience, prayer in practice meets obstacles that a theoretical discussion too easily glosses over and forgets. Even when prayer is defined as communion with God, and our thought of it is thereby freed from many embarrassments, as a kite escapes the trees and bushes when one flies it high, there remain practical difficulties which perplex many who sincerely try to pray.

For example, real communion involves the vivid consciousness that someone is present, with whom we are enjoying fellowship. Now a man may believe that God is, may desire earnestly to speak with him, and may not doubt in theory the possibility of such communion; but in practice he may utterly fail to feel the presence of God. In spite of his best efforts he may seem to himself to be talking into empty space. The sense of futility—such as comes to one who finds that he has been speaking in the dark to nobody, when he supposed a friend was in the room—may so confuse him that, theory or no theory, prayer becomes practically valueless. He cries with Job, not in a spirit of scepticism, but in great perplexity and in genuine desire for the divine fellowship, "Behold, I go forward, but he is not there; And backward, but I cannot perceive him" (Job 23:8). The practice of God's presence is not so simple as words sometimes make it seem.

One obvious reason for this sense of God's unreality, which often makes helpful prayer impossible, lies of course in *character*. Isaiah was dealing with a universal truth when he said: "Your iniquities have separated between you and your God, and your sins have hid his face from you" (Isaiah 59:2). One has only to consider that frivolous American who in the Rembrandt room of the Amsterdam Gallery looked lackadaisically around and asked: "I wonder if there is anything here worth seeing"; one has only to recall the women who climbed an Alpine height on an autumn day, when the riot of color in the valley sobered into the green of the pines upon the heights, and over all stood the crests of eternal snow, and who inquired in the full sight of all this, "We heard there was a view up here; where is it?" to see that there is a spiritual qualification for every experience, and that without it nothing fine and beautiful can ever be real to any one. "Mr. Turner," a man once said to the artist, "I never see any sunsets like yours." And the artist answered grimly, "No, sir. Don't you wish you could?" How clearly then must the sense of God's reality be a progressive and often laborious achievement of the spirit! It is not a matter to be taken for granted, as though any one could saunter into God's presence at any time, in any mood, with any sort of life behind him, and at once perceive God there.

Let some debauché from the dens of a city walk into a company where men are chivalrous and women pure, and how much will the debauché understand of his new environment? Stone walls are not so impenetrable as the veil of moral difference between the clean and unclean. So spiritual alienation between God and man makes fellowship impossible. Of all the evils that most surely work this malign result in man's communion with the Father, the Master specially noted two: *impurity*—"Blessed are the pure in heart, for *they* shall see God"; and *vindictiveness,* the unbrotherly spirit that will not forgive nor seek to be forgiven—"If therefore thou art offering thy gift before the altar, and there rememberest that thy brother hath ought against thee, leave there thy gift before the altar, and go thy way, first be reconciled to thy brother, and then come and offer thy gift" (Matt. 5:23, 24). *No one can be wrong with man and right with God.* In Coleridge's "Ancient Mariner," one of the most vivid pictures of sin's consequences ever drawn, the effect of lovelessness on prayer is put into a rememberable verse:

> "I looked to heaven and tried to pray,
>   But or ever a prayer had gush't,
> A wicked whisper came and made
>   My heart as dry as dust."

Most of us have experienced that stanza's truth. The harboring of a grudge, the subtle wish for another's harm, the envy that corrupts the heart, even if it find no expression in word or deed—such attitudes always prove impassable barriers to spontaneous prayer. When, therefore, any one encounters the practical difficulty that arises from the sense of God's unreality, he may well search his life for sinister habits of thought, for cherished evils dimly recognized as wrong but unsurrendered, for lax carelessness in conduct or deliberate infidelity to conscience, for sins whose commission he deplores, but whose results he still clings to and desires, and above all for selfishness that hinders loving and so breaks the connections that bind us to God and one another.

II

The sense of God's unreality, however, does not necessarily imply a wicked life. There are other reasons which often hinder men from a vivid consciousness of God. All of us, for example, have *moods* in which the vision of God grows dim. Our life is not built on a level so that we can maintain a constant elevation of spirit. We have mountains and valleys, emotional ups and downs; and, as with our Lord, the radiant experience of transfiguration is succeeded by an hour of bitterness when the soul cries, "My God, my God, why hast thou forsaken me?" (Matt. 27:46). Cowper tells us that in prayer he had known such exaltation that he thought he would die from excess of joy; but at another time, asked for some hymns for a new hymnal, he wrote in answer, "How can you ask of me such a service? I seem to myself to be banished to a remoteness from God's presence, in comparison with which the distance from the East to the West is vicinity, is cohesion." Of course we cannot always pray with the same intensity and conscious satisfaction. "I pray more heartily at some times than at others," says Tolstoi; and even Bunyan had his familiar difficulties: "O, the starting holes that the heart hath in the time of prayer! None knows how many by-ways the heart hath and back lanes to slip away from the presence of God." The first step in dealing with this familiar experience is to recognize its naturalness and therefore to go through it undismayed. When Paul said to Timothy, "Be urgent in season, out of season," he was giving that advice which a wise experience always gives to immaturity: Make up your mind in advance to keep your course steady, *when you feel like it and when you don't*. This difficulty of moods has been met by all God's people. The biography of any spiritual leader contains passages such as this, from one of Hugh Latimer's letters to his fellow-martyr, Ridley: "Pardon me and pray for me; pray for me, I say. For I am sometimes so fearful, that I would creep into a mouse-hole; sometimes God doth visit me again with his comfort. So he cometh and goeth."

A man who surrenders to these variable moods is doomed to inefficiency. He is like a ship that drifts as the tides run and the winds blow, and does not hold its course through them and in spite of them. Matthew Arnold goes to the pith of the problem, so far as duty-doing is concerned:

> "tasks in hours of insight willed
> Can be in hours of gloom fulfilled."

And the same attitude is necessary in the life of prayer. Of course we cannot always pray with the same sense of God's nearness, the

same warmth of conscious fellowship with him. Plotinus said that
he had *really* prayed only four times in his life. Lowell, in his
"Cathedral," writes,

> "I that still pray at morning and at eve . . .
> Thrice in my life perhaps have truly prayed,
> Thrice, stirred below my conscious self, have felt
> That perfect disenthralment which is God."

The heights of fellowship with God are not often reached—even the
record of Jesus' life contains only one Transfiguration—but this
does not mean that the value of prayer is only thus occasional. As
Dean Goulburn put it, *"When you cannot pray as you would, pray
as you can."* A man does not deny the existence of the sun because
it is a cloudy day, nor cease to count on the sun to serve him and his.
Moods are the clouds in our spiritual skies. A man must not over-
emphasize their importance. Surely he should not on account of
them cease to trust the God who is temporarily obscured by them.

Moreover, a man need not passively allow his moods to become
chronic. Many a life, like an old-fashioned well, has latent resources
of living water underneath, but the pump needs priming. Into a
man's prayerless mood let a little living water from some one else's
prayer be poured, and water from the nether wells of the man's own
soul may flow again. For such a purpose, collections of prayers like
the Bishop of Ripon's "The Communion of Prayer" or Tileston's
"Great Souls at Prayer" are useful; and books of devotion such as
St. Augustine's "Confessions." They often prime the pump. Indeed,
prayer itself is a great conqueror of perverse moods. You are not in
the spirit of prayer and therefore will refuse to pray until your mood
chances to be congenial? But clearly Dr. Forsyth's comparison is
apt: "Sometimes when you need rest most you are too restless to lie
down and take it. Then compel yourself to lie down and to lie still.
Often in ten minutes the compulsion fades into consent and you
sleep, and rise a new man . . . So if you are averse to pray, pray
the more."

III

Deeper than the difficulty of passing moods lies the problem of
those who *habitually* fail to feel the presence of God. In many cases

the trouble is *temperamental*. Some men seem by their native con-
stitution to be specially designed for religion. They are geniuses in
the realm of spirit, as a Beethoven is in music or a Raphael in art.
The unseen is real to them; they are immediately aware of its
presence, sensitive to its meaning, responsive to its appeal. When they
speak of prayer their vivid experience of God demands for its expression poetry rather than prose. "Orison," they cry with Mech-
thild of Magdeburg, "draws the great God into he small heart; it
drives the hungry soul out to the full God. It brings together two
lovers, God and the soul, into a joyful room." To temperaments of
this quality the practice of God's presence is as spontaneous as any
human love and quite as real.

But what of one who is not thus gifted? He is perhaps of a
practical temperament, a man of action rather than of meditation.
Even in human relationships he is not demonstrative, and is more
given to revealing his loyalty and affection by concrete deeds of
service than by radiant hours of communion. He stands perplexed
before the exalted moods of the mystic. He cannot so strain himself
as to reach them. He feels out of his element when he reads about
them. When he prays he reaches no heights of conscious fellowship
with God. During the singing of a hymn like "Sweet Hour of
Prayer" he feels as unresponsive to the experience from which the
hymn arose as Dean Stanley would have felt to the music. The Dean
could not recognize even the national anthem save by the fact that
the people all arose at the first bar. What shall be said to a man who
thus believes in God and tries to do his will, but who is not warmly
conscious of fellowship with him in prayer? Something surely must
be said, for if prayer is so interpreted that it is left as the possession
of those only who are of the emotional and mystic temperament,
many of the most useful folk on earth, in whom practical and intellectual interests are supreme—the thinkers and the workers—will
feel themselves excluded from the possibility of praying.

We touch here one of the most crucial matters in our study of
prayer. *Every man must be allowed to pray in his own way.* It is far
from being true that the most valuable temperament in religion is
the mystical. God needs us all. Some are phlegmatic—stolid, patient,
undemonstrative; some are choleric—high-spirited, nervous, passionate; some are sanguine—hopeful, cheerful, light-hearted; some
are somber and serious. Even this time-honored classification of the
temperaments is not exhaustive. There are as many temperaments

as there are men, and each has his own problems and his peculiar
way of expressing the spirit of Christ. The first step in useful living
for many folk is the recognition of God's purpose in making us on
such unique and individual plans. He evidently likes us better that
way. John makes a better John than Peter ever could have been, and
Peter a more useful Peter than was possible to John. We are so used
to school examinations where the whole class must submit to the
same tests of excellence that we forget how surely in the moral life
we shall have individual tests. Each man is being tried in a private
examination. He is not expected to be a Christian in any other man's
way. As in Emerson's parable of the mountain and the squirrel, he
can be undismayed by the special excellence of another, and can say
as the squirrel did to the mountain,

> "If I cannot carry forests on my back,
> Neither can you crack a nut."

Now this general principle has its special application to prayer.
*Nothing could be more intensely individual than the prayers of the
Bible.* Nobody tries to commune with God in any one else's way.
Some pray kneeling, like Paul (Acts 20:36); some standing, like
Jeremiah (Jer. 18:20); some sitting, like David (II Sam. 7:18);
some prostrate, like Jesus (Matt. 26:39). Some pray silently, like
Hannah (I Sam. 1:13); some aloud, like Ezekiel (Ezek. 11:13).
Some pray in the temple (II Kings 19:14); some in bed (Psalm
63:6), in the fields (Gen. 24:11, 12), on the hillside (Gen. 28:18-
20), on the battlefield (I Sam. 7:5), by a riverside (Acts 16:13), on
the seashore (Acts 21:5), in the privacy of the chamber (Matt.
6:6). Moreover all sorts of temperaments are found at prayer;
practical leaders like Nehemiah, who in a silent ejaculation of the
spirit seeks God's help before he speaks to the king (Neh. 1:3, 5);
poets like the writer of the twenty-seventh Psalm, who love communion with God; men of melancholy mind like Jeremiah, "Hast
thou utterly rejected Judah? hath thy soul loathed Zion?" (Jer.
14:19); and men of radiant spirit like Isaiah, "Jehovah, even
Jehovah, is my strength and song; and he is become my salvation"
(Isaiah 12:2). *There are as many different ways of praying as there
are different individuals.* Consider the prayer of St. Augustine: "Let
my soul take refuge from the crowding turmoil of worldly thoughts
beneath the shadow of thy wings; let my heart, this sea of restless

waves, find peace in thee, O God." And then in contrast consider the prayer of Lord Ashley, before he charged at the battle of Edge Hill: "O Lord, thou knowest how busy I must be this day. If I forget thee, do not thou forget me."

We need always to remember, therefore, that there is no one mould of prayer into which our communion with God must be run. Let each man pray as best he can. Let no man make himself the slave of another's methods. Professor George Albert Coe has put a valuable truth into a few succinct sentences: "The tendency . . . is to create an impression that the more valuable forms of prayer are reserved for a special class of persons. This impression, too, is unconsciously fostered by the adulation that is bestowed upon men, often young men, who cultivate a particular type of prayer, and talk a great deal about it. What we need more than almost anything else is to cultivate in timid souls that tend to self-distrust, in critical souls that think before they assert, and in active souls that prefer giving to receiving, a robust respect for their own natural types of prayer."

IV

If we are to deal adequately, however, with the trouble which some habitually and all of us occasionally have in realizing the presence of God, we must do more than tell each man to pray as he can. There are prevalent attitudes among people who try to pray that make the consciousness of God's presence well-nigh impossible. We may note as the first of these that *vague groping after a God outside of us which so often ends in the futile feeling of having talked to empty space.* Many men, in their earnest desire to enter fully into the Christian experience, strain after a realization of God's presence as though by some violence and stress of the will it could be attained. Their souls are mortars, their petitions bombs; they explode themselves toward heaven, and save for the echo of their own outburst they hear no answer whatever. Madame Guyon records that just this was her perplexity until a Franciscan friar gave her this suggestive advice: "Madame, you are seeking *without* that which you have *within*. Accustom yourself to seek God in your own heart, and you will find him." This counsel is wise and practical. The presence of God can be *experienced* only within our own hearts. *All the best in us is God in us.* Generally, if not always, it is quite impossible to distinguish between the voice of God and the voice of our own best conscience and ideals. They are not to be distinguished. What we call conscience and ideals *are* God's voice, mediated to us through our own finest endowments.

This does not mean that these voices of God, mediated to us through our best, are infallible. It does mean that God in them is trying to speak to us according to our capacity to understand. If our windows are soiled, the sun's rays are hindered; but that fact is no denial of the truth that whatever light does come through our windows comes from the sun. So God is compelled to minister his blessing to us through our own capacities to receive and appropriate. *No man should ever grope outside of his best self to find God. He should always seek the God who is speaking to him in his best self.*

During a dry season in the New Hebrides, John G. Paton the missionary awakened the derision of the natives by digging for water. They said water always came down from heaven, not up through the earth. But Paton revealed a larger truth than they had seen before by discovering to them that heaven could give them water through their own land. So men insist on waiting for God to send them blessing in some supernormal way, when all the while he is giving them abundant supply if they would only learn to retreat into the fertile places of their own spirits where, as Jesus said, the wells of living waters seek to rise. We need to learn Eckhart's lesson, "God is nearer to me than I am to myself; he is just as near to wood and stone, but they do not know it." We need to understand the word attributed to Albert the Great, "To mount to God is to enter into one's self. For he who inwardly entereth and intimately penetrateth into himself gets above and beyond himself and truly mounts up to God." And in learning the meaning of words like these, we shall be coming into the spirit of many a Scripture passage: "If we love one another, God *abideth in us*" (I John 4:12); "We are a temple of the living God; even as God said, I will *dwell in them*" (II Cor. 6:16); "If any man . . . open the door, I will *come in* to him, and will sup with him, and he with me" (Rev. 3:20); "The water that I shall give him shall become *in him* a well of water" (John 4:14).

Any one, therefore, troubled by the seeming unreality of God may well imitate the Psalmist who begins his psalm by saying, "I will cry unto God," and who in the sixth verse says, "I commune with mine own heart" (Psalm 77). The two verses are not in conflict. The only way any one can commune with God is *through* his own heart. Indeed, we may call those psychologists to witness who discover in the spirit's life the transforming influences of which we have been speaking, and who ascribe them to the "subconscious." Powers of joy and peace, influences that renovate character, change disposition, and inspire service, do appear in human life, they say, but these effects which the New Testament attributes to the Holy Spirit, they ascribe to the "subconscious." There should be no permanent misunderstanding here. The tides that come into New York Harbor come through the Narrows, but they do not start there. You never can get at the secret of the inflow from the sea, which makes the sailing of great ships possible, by saying that the presence of the Narrows explains it. The tides come *through* the Narrows, not *from* them. So we cannot solve the mystery of that divine help which great souls know by giving names to substations in our own minds. We must go deeper and farther than that. *God himself is trying through our best to find a channel for his Spirit.*

v

The consideration of this vague groping after a God outside of us, leads us to a matter even more important. The elemental trouble with the prayers of those who fail to find God real is often the very fact that they are *seeking for God.* No one is prepared to experience the presence of God until he sees that *God is seeking for him.* Paul describes the pagan world as seeking God, "if haply they might feel after him and find him" (Acts 17:27); and many a Christian in this regard is a pagan still. We have turned the parables of Jesus in the fifteenth Chapter of Luke quite upside down. According to our attitude in prayer, the shepherd is lost, and the sheep have gone out on the tempest-driven mountainside to hunt for him. But not so the Master! To him the sheep are wandering, and the shepherd with undiscourageable persistency is seeking them. Without this thought of God as initiating the search, so that our finding of him is simply our response to his quest for us, the endeavor of any man to seek God is of all enterprises the most hopeless. How can the finite discover the Infinite unless the Infinite desires to be found? How can man break up into an experience of God unless God is seeking to reach down into friendship with man? *The deepest necessity of a fruitful life of prayer is the recognition that God's search for men is prior to any man's search for God.* In the words of one of Faber's hymns,

> " 'Tis rather God who seeks for us
>   Than we who seek for him."

Now the search of God for man has always been believed by Christians, but by many it has become a historical matter. God *did* seek for man in Christ. This fundamental truth is of the utmost importance for prayer. For, as a matter of fact, whenever a Christian prays he prays to the God whose love for us Christ revealed, and to the knowledge of whom we never should have come without Christ. As Fichte put it, "All who since Jesus have come into union with God have come unto union with God *through him.*" But this belief in God's search for man in Christ is not sufficient for prayer. *God is forever seeking each man.* The promptings of conscience, the lure of fine ideals, the demands of friendship, the suggestions of good books, the calls to service, every noble impulse in hours when

> "The spirit's true endowments
>   Stand out plainly from the false ones,"

are all the approach of God to us. Prayer is not groping after him Prayer is opening the life up to him. The prayerless heart is fleeing from God. Finding God is really letting God find us; for our search for him is simply surrender to his search for us. When the truth of this is clearly seen, prayer becomes real. There is no more talking into empty space, no more fumbling in the dark to lay hold on him. We go into the secret place and there let every fine and ennobling influence which God is sending to us have free play. We let him speak to us through our best thoughts, our clearest spiritual visions, our finest conscience. We no longer endeavor to escape. We find him as run-away children, weary of their escapade, find their father. *They consent to be found by him.*

> "I said, 'I will find God,' and forth I went
>   To seek Him in the clearness of the sky,
>   But over me stood unendurably
>   Only a pitiless, sapphire firmament
> Ringing the world, blank splendour; yet intent
>   Still to find God, 'I will go seek,' said I,
>   'His way upon the waters,' and drew nigh
>   An ocean marge, weed-strewn and foam-besprent;

And the waves dashed on idle sand and stone,
  And very vacant was the long, blue sea;
But in the evening as I sat alone,
My window open to the vanishing day,
Dear God! I could not chóose but kneel and pray,
  And it sufficed that I was found of Thee."[1]

SUGGESTIONS FOR THOUGHT AND DISCUSSION

Why do most people find it hard to pray?

In how far are the types of hindrances which prevent communion with God peculiar to the "realm of religion"?

What is necessary to be able to enjoy a sunset, a painting, or a musical symphony? Can any but a technical expert really enjoy these? To what extent do these conclusions apply to enjoying communion with God?

Can a man without an appreciation of nature, art and intellectual integrity fully commune with God? How far is the completeness of such communion dependent upon the range of human interests and experiences?

In the light of the above questions, to what extent are "spiritual" qualifications essential only to "religious" experiences?

How do the hindrances to human friendship differ from the hindrances to communion with God?

In the light of Jesus' teachings, what are the principal hindrances to prayer in the realm of character?

Where first shall we look for hindrances to communion with God?

What dependence is to be placed upon "favorable moods"?

In the general enterprises of human life, how much allowance is made for favorable moods?

How far is special application necessary if advantage is to be taken of such moods? What is the relation of favorable moods to prayer? What light does the Transfiguration throw on this?

[1]Edward Dowden.

*What relation has a man's temperament to his ability to achieve
    reality in prayer?*

How far is reality in prayer possible to people with other than a
mystical temperament? What proportion of prayers recorded in the
Bible are the prayers of mystics? What proportion in later history?

To what degree must the form of prayer be determined by the
type of personality? What answer would the Bible record of prayers
suggest?

What prevalent attitudes among the people make the consciousness of God's presence well-nigh impossible? How can these attitudes
be overcome?

*How can the hindrances to prayer in the life of any particular in-
    dividual be overcome?*

CHAPTER VI

Prayer and the Reign of Law

DAILY READINGS

First Day, Sixth Week

The heavens declare the glory of God;
And the firmament showeth his handiwork.
Day unto day uttereth speech,
And night unto night showeth knowledge.
There is no speech nor language;
Their voice is not heard.
Their line is gone out through all the earth,
And their words to the end of the world.
In them hath he set a tabernacle for the sun,
Which is as a bridegroom coming out of his chamber,
And rejoiceth as a strong man to run his course.
His going forth is from the end of the heavens,
And his circuit unto the ends of it;
And there is nothing hid from the heat thereof.
—Psalm 19:1-6.

Consider the ease with which the Psalmist here ascribes all the activities of the heavens to the direct influence of God. The idea of natural law has not gotten between him and the Creator; whenever the sun comes up or the stars appear he feels that God is doing it. Now it may still be true, as Mr. Chesterton remarks, that each morning God says to the sun, "Get up, do it again!" but it is difficult for most people to imagine that. The sun seems to *run itself by law;* everything seems to run itself, so that in the modern mind this psalm is unconsciously changed until it reads, "The heavens declare the glory of *law.*" In the weekly comment we shall consider the un-reasonableness of this negation of religious faith which our modern scientific knowledge has caused in many, but in the daily readings let us note *the ways in which our new information about natural law practically affects us.* Does it not, as we have today suggested, seem to push God away off? The world looks like a great machine, self-running and self-regulating, with God a very distant Sustainer, if he is anywhere at all. Thomas Hood put the feeling into a familiar verse:

> "I remember, I remember
>   The fir-trees dark and high;
> I used to think their slender tops
>   Were close against the sky.
> It was a childish ignorance,
>   But now 'tis little joy
> To know I'm farther off from heaven
>   Than when I was a boy."

O God, we thank Thee for this universe, our great home; for its vastness and its riches, and for the manifoldness of the life which teems upon it and of which we are part. We praise Thee for the arching sky and the blessed winds, for the driving clouds and the constellations on high. We praise Thee for the salt sea and the running water, for the everlasting hills, for the trees, and for the grass under our feet. We thank Thee for our senses by which we can see the splendor of the morning, and hear the jubilant songs of love, and smell the breath of the springtime. Grant us, we pray Thee, a heart wide open to all this joy and beauty, and save our souls from being so steeped in care or so darkened by passion that we pass heedless and unseeing when even the thornbush by the wayside is aflame with the glory of God.—Walter Rauschenbusch.

Second Day, Sixth Week

O Jehovah, thou hast searched me, and known me.
Thou knowest my downsitting and mine uprising;
Thou understandest my thought afar off.
Thou searchest out my path and my lying down,
And art acquainted with all my ways.

For there is not a word in my tongue,
But, lo, O Jehovah, thou knowest it altogether.
Thou hast beset me behind and before,
And laid thy hand upon me.
Such knowledge is too wonderful for me;
It is high, I cannot attain unto it.
Whither shall I go from thy Spirit?
Or whither shall I flee from thy presence?
If I ascend up into heaven, thou art there;
If I make my bed in Sheol, behold, thou art there.
If I take the wings of the morning,
And dwell in the uttermost parts of the sea;
Even there shall thy hand lead me.—Psalm 139:1-10.

In contrast with this Psalmist's sense of God's immediate presence, the reign of law not only seems to push God away off; it pushes him away back into history. He becomes nothing more than a hypothesis to explain how the universe happened to exist in the first place. In President Faunce's figure, men think of God as an engineer who started this locomotive of a world, pulled the throttle wide open, and then leaped from the cab; and the world has been running its own unguided course ever since on the rails of law.

This does not simply make impossible the spiritual faith which glows in our Scripture passage; it violates every canon of sound thinking. It is childish. It is on a par with the belief of the Piedmontese peasant, of whom Benjamin Constant tells. He thought that the world was made by a God who had died before his work was completed. Consider whether your prayers have been hindered by the subtle influence of this idea of God. Before men can really pray, God must be seen as the present *living* God—whose ways of action we partially have plotted and called laws.

O Lord, our God, we desire to feel Thee near us in spirit and in body at this time. We know that in Thee we live and move and have our being, but we are cast down and easily disquieted, and we wander in many a sad wilderness where we lose the conscious experience of Thy presence. Yet the deepest yearning of our hearts is unto Thee. As the hart panteth after the waterbrooks, so pant our souls after Thee, O God. Nothing less than Thyself can still the hunger, or quench the thirst with which Thou hast inspired us.

Power of our souls! enter Thou into them and fit them for Thyself,
making them pure with Christ's purity, loving and lovable with His
love.—Samuel McComb.

Third Day, Sixth Week

And in like manner the Spirit also helpeth our infirmity: for we
know not how to pray as we ought; but the Spirit himself maketh
intercession for us with groanings which cannot be uttered; and he
that searcheth the hearts knoweth what is the mind of the Spirit,
because he maketh intercession for the saints according to the will
of God. And we know that to them that love God all things work
together for good, even to them that are called according to his
purpose.—Romans 8:26-28.

Note the connection of thought here between *prayer,* and *belief in*
the controlling providence of God that makes all things work together for good to those that love him. Is not this connection vital?
Unless God's providence does control, so that he is now at work in
the world shaping events and moulding men, what is the use of
praying? But just here is one of our modern perplexities. *The reign*
of law seems to rule out the activity of Providence. When we were
children, many of us doubtless prayed as Florence Nightingale said
she did. "When I was young," she writes, "I could not understand
what people meant by 'their thoughts wandering in prayer.' I asked
for what I really wished, and really wished for what I asked. And
my thoughts wandered no more than those of a mother would
wander, who was supplicating her Sovereign for her son's reprieve
from execution. . . . I liked the morning service much better than
the afternoon, because we asked for more things. . . . I was always
miserable if I was not at church when the Litany was said. How ill-
natured it is, if you believe in prayer, not to ask for everybody what
they want. . . . I could not pray for George IV. I thought the
people very good who prayed for him, and wondered whether he
could have been much worse if he had not been prayed for. William
IV I prayed for a little. But when Victoria came to the throne, I
prayed for her in a rapture of feeling and my thoughts never
wandered."

What is it that has changed this childlike spirit in our prayers? Is
it not our increasing knowledge of the reign of natural law? So

Miss Nightingale came to say in contrast with her childhood's point of view, "God's scheme for us is not that he should give us what we ask for, but that mankind should obtain it for mankind." Consider the people whom you know who have altogether given up praying for this same reason.

Almighty God, of Thy fulness grant to us who need so much, who lack so much, who have so little, wisdom and strength. Bring our wills unto Thine. Lift our understandings into Thy heavenly light; that we thereby beholding those things which are right, and being drawn by Thy love, may bring our will and our understanding together to Thy service, until at last, body and soul and spirit may be all Thine, and Thou be our Father and our Eternal Friend. Amen. George Dawson (1821-1876).

Fourth Day, Sixth Week

Bless Jehovah, O my soul.
O Jehovah, my God, thou art very great;
Thou art clothed with honor and majesty:
Who coveredst thyself with light as with a garment;
Who stretchest out the heavens like a curtain;
Who layeth the beams of his chambers in the waters;
Who maketh the clouds his chariot;
Who walketh upon the wings of the wind;
Who maketh winds his messengers;
Flames of fire his ministers;
Who laid the foundations of the earth,
That it should not be moved for ever.
Thou coveredst it with the deep as with a vesture;
The waters stood above the mountains.
At thy rebuke they fled;
At the voice of thy thunder they hasted away
(The mountains rose, the valleys sank down)
Unto the place which thou hadst founded for them.
Thou hast set a bound that they may not pass over;
That they turn not again to cover the earth.
He sendeth forth springs into the valleys;
They run among the mountains;
They give drink to every beast of the field;

The wild asses quench their thirst.
By them the birds of the heavens have their habitation;
They sing among the branches.—Psalm 104:1-12.

Read the entire Psalm, a glowing expression of faith in the controlling presence of God in his world. Now in our day many are
troubled in their endeavor to share such a faith, because the reign
of law suggests that any help from God would involve a *miracle,*
an intervention in the regular, natural order. How can God shape
the course of nature and human history without *interfering with
law?* But consider that what we call a miracle need not involve at
all a break in any law. Plant a pebble and a seed side by side. The
law of the pebble is to lie dead; the law of the seed is to grow. If
therefore the pebble could see the seed sprouting, how certainly it
would lift its pebble hands in astonishment and cry, "A miracle!"
But no law is broken there. There and everywhere else, what is
called miracle is not a rupture of law; *it is the fulfilling of a larger
and higher law than we have yet understood.* God's providence
never has and never does involve breaking his laws; it means that
we are as little acquainted with all the resources of the spiritual universe as a pebble is with the resources of a plant, and that God
guides the course of events by means of laws, some of which are
known to us and some unknown. Remember that natural law is
nothing but man's statement of how things regularly happen, *so far
as he has been able to observe them.* What looks like a miracle to
man is no miracle to God. To him it is as natural as sunrise.

*O Lord God, in whom we live, and move, and have our being,
open our eyes that we may behold Thy Fatherly presence ever about
us. Draw our hearts to Thee with the power of Thy love. Teach us
to be anxious for nothing, and when we have done what Thou hast
given us to do, help us, O God our Saviour, to leave the issue to Thy
wisdom. Take from us all doubt and mistrust. Lift our thoughts up
to Thee in heaven, and make us to know that all things are possible
to us through Thy Son our Redeemer. Amen.*—Bishop Westcott.

Fifth Day, Sixth Week

It is he that sitteth above the circle of the earth, and the inhabit-
ants thereof are as grasshoppers; that stretcheth out the heavens

as a curtain, and spreadeth them out as a tent to dwell in; that
bringeth princes to nothing; that maketh the judges of the earth
as vanity. Yea, they have not been planted; yea, they have not been
sown; yea, their stock hath not taken root in the earth: moreover
he bloweth upon them, and they wither, and the whirlwind taketh
them away as stubble. To whom then will ye liken me, that I should
be equal to him? saith the Holy One. Lift up your eyes on high, and
see who hath created these, that bringeth out their host by number;
he calleth them all by name; by the greatness of his might, and for
that he is strong in power, not one is lacking.—Isaiah 40:22-26.

The central trouble in the religious thinking of many people lies
here: *the new knowledge of the universe has made their childish
thoughts of God inadequate, and instead of getting a worthier and
larger idea of God to meet the new need, they give up all vital
thought about God whatsoever.* We can feel Isaiah in this fortieth
chapter reaching out for as great a conception of God as he can
compass, because the situation demands it. Our modern situation
calls for the same outreach of mind. This is the truth behind Sam
Foss's poem:

> "A boy was born 'mid little things,
>   Between a little world and sky,
> And dreamed not of the cosmic rings
>   'Round which the circling planets fly.

> "He lived in little works and thoughts,
>   Where little ventures grow and plod,
> And paced and ploughed his little plots,
>   And prayed unto his little God.

> "But, as the mighty system grew,
>   His faith grew faint with many scars;
> The cosmos widened in his view,
>   But God was lost among his stars.

> "Another boy in lowly days,
>   As he, to little things was born,
> But gathered lore in woodland ways,
>   And from the glory of the morn.

"As wider skies broke on his view,
    God greatened in his growing mind;
Each year he dreamed his God anew,
    And left his older God behind.

"He saw the boundless scheme dilate,
    In star and blossom, sky and clod;
And, as the universe grew great,
    He dreamed for it a greater God."

O God our Father, who dost exhort us to pray, and who dost grant what we ask, if only, when we ask, we live a better life; hear me, who am trembling in this darkness, and stretch forth Thy hand unto me; hold forth Thy light before me; recall me from my wanderings; and, Thou being my Guide, may I be restored to myself and to Thee, through Jesus Christ. Amen.—St. Augustine (354-430).

Sixth Day, Sixth Week

For though the fig-tree shall not flourish,
Neither shall fruit be in the vines;
The labor of the olive shall fail,
And the fields shall yield no food;
The flock shall be cut off from the fold,
And there shall be no herd in the stalls:
Yet I will rejoice in Jehovah,
I will joy in the God of my salvation.
                    —Habakkuk 3:17, 18.

We have noted five effects that knowledge of the reign of law has on modern minds: it pushes God away off; pushes him away back; makes his special help seem impossible; suggests that any providential aid would involve a miracle; and finally makes our immature, childish ideas of him inadequate. But now supposing that all of these were overcome, and that like Habakkuk, a man believed thoroughly in the providential control of a living God in his world—note the lack of presumption with which he uses his faith. The forces of nature are in the hands of God, but the prophet does not immodestly demand that they shall be used in accordance with human desire. It may even be that they bring dire trouble on him, as the seventeenth verse pictures; yet he does not doubt the guidance of God in the world. Consider the importance of this attitude for prayer. Belief in God's providence is not to be confused with the arrogant assumption that that providence must be exercised as we wish. One summer in England when the clergy were vehemently praying for dry weather, Charles Kingsley refused to do so. "How do we know," he said in a sermon, "that in praying God to take away these rains, we are not-asking him to send the cholera in the year to come? I am of opinion that we are . . . Now, perhaps you may understand better why I said that I was afraid of being presumptuous in praying for fine weather."

O Thou, who givest liberally, unto all men and upbraidest not, give to this, Thy servant, the desire of his heart. Thou knowest his inward and outward state. Whatever it be that holds him back from self-surrender, unto Thee, grant that it may be taken out of the way, that there may be a free and open intercourse between him and Thee. May he be willing to trust where he cannot prove; willing to believe his better moments in spite of all that contradicts them. Open his eyes to see Thee as Thou art, infinitely real, infinitely gracious, infinitely good. Speak to him in the daily witness of earth and sky; in the goodness and tender mercy of human hearts; above all, in the words and works of Thy perfect Son in whom Thou hast spoken the "everlasting yea" that puts to flight our every care. Take from him all dread of evils that may never happen. Grant him the victory over every besetting doubt; and patience while any darkness remains, that he may glorify Thee, through Jesus Christ our Lord. Amen.—Samuel McComb.

Seventh Day, Sixth Week

I will give thee thanks with my whole heart:
Before the gods will I sing praises unto thee.
I will worship toward thy holy temple,
And give thanks unto thy name for thy lovingkindness and for thy
    truth:
For thou hast magnified thy word above all thy name.
In the day that I called thou answeredst me,
Thou didst encourage me with strength in my soul . . .
Though I walk in the midst of trouble, thou wilt revive me;

Thou wilt stretch forth thy hand against the wrath of mine enemies,
And thy right hand will save me.
Jehovah will perfect that which concerneth me:
Thy lovingkindness, O Jehovah, endureth for ever.
                                    —Psalm 138:1-3, 7, 8.

Note the joyful certainty with which this Psalmist testifies to the
effect of prayer on his own life. With all the puzzles that perplex our
thought when we try to pray that God will change outward circumstances, this inward realm where prayer is continually efficacious remains undisturbed. Read thoughtfully this testimony from Henry M.
Stanley, the African explorer: "To relate a little of the instances in
my life wherein I have been grateful for the delicate monitions of an
inner voice, recalling me, as it were, to 'my true self,' it would be
difficult for me to do their importance justice. I, for one, must not,
dare not, say that prayers are inefficacious. Where I have been
earnest, I have been answered. . . . In the conduct of the various
expeditions into Africa, prayer for patience has enabled me to view
my savage opponents in a humorous light; sometimes with infinite
compassion for their madness. . . . Without prayer for it, I doubt
that I could have endured the flourish of the spears when they were
but half-a-dozen paces off. . . . On all my expeditions prayer made
me stronger, morally and mentally, than any of my non-praying companions. It did not blind my eyes, or dull my mind, or close my ears;
but, on the contrary, it gave me confidence. It did more; it gave me
joy and pride in my work, and lifted me hopefully over the one
thousand five hundred miles of forest tracks, eager to face the day's
perils and fatigues."

*Eternal God, lead us into the blessedness of the mystery of com-
munion with Thee. Bow our spirits in deepest reverence before
Thee, yet uplift us into a sense of kinship. Send the spirit of Thy
Son into our hearts, crying "Abba Father," that all unworthy fear
may be banished by the gladness of Thy perfect love. Thy love is
like the luminous heaven, receiving only to purify the foulest breath
of earth. Thy gentleness is like the sun, seeking to cheer and warm
the chilled hearts of men. Touch us, O our Father, with a feeling
of Thy great realities, for though our thought about Thee is better
than our words, our experience of Thee is better than our thought.*—
Samuel McComb.

COMMENT FOR THE WEEK

I

One element in communion with God has so far been kept in the background of our discussion. Prayer is conversation, but generally it is not merely conversation for conversation's sake. Sometimes we talk with our friends for the sheer joy of talking, but sometimes we talk because we want something. So communion with God is commonly motivated by desire; *the element of petition belongs by nature to the tendency which has led all men to pray.* Now, as soon as petition enters into a man's prayers, he is likely to run against an obstacle that seems very formidable. He comes face to face with the reign of law, as modern knowledge has revealed it.

In a world where there is a cause for every effect and an effect for every cause, where each event is intermeshed with every other and all move by inevitable consequence from what has gone before, it seems absurd to expect God to change anything in answer to our call. Men feel this when they consider the vastness of the universe throughout which the unbroken reign of law obtains. If the ring upon a girl's finger be taken as the orbit of the earth, 180,000,000 miles in diameter, the nearest star is one and a half miles away; the mass of the heavenly bodies scores of hundreds of miles beyond that, and throughout the whole expanse law is absolute. Or if one looks at near-by things to rest his thought from such iron regularity, he finds no comfort there. Of all snow-crystals that ever fell, there have been no angles of crystallization in their filaments except 60° and 120°. The wind is as obedient to law as is a falling stone; the temperature of the air is as much a creature of cause and effect as is the rising sun; and the rays of radium, infinitesimally minute and so swift that one could encompass the earth thrice in a single second and still have time to spare, are as regular in their law-abiding ways as an eclipse.

Indeed, if one look within himself, in hope of evading law, he fails. The mind's operations too are controlled by laws, and the psychologists are plotting them with increasing accuracy. The conviction irresistibly claims our assent that nothing happens anywhere contrary to law. The conditions which cause an Aurora Borealis are not fully known, but no one doubts that the conditions exist, and that if they fail by the least degree an Aurora cannot be conjured up by all the prayers of all the saints on earth. Definite petition to God in such a world seems absurd. To many even communion with God grows difficult, so lost is he in the maze of law. Job's cry gains strength a thousandfold today—"O that I knew where I might find him!" (Job 23:3). As for the demand that we continue to pray *without* understanding, self-respect rebels. Otway's words in "Venice Preserved," though written in 1682, have a contemporary ring in them:

> "You want to lead
> My reason blindfold like a hampered lion,
> Check'd of his noble vigour—then, when baited
> Down to obedient tameness, may it couch
> And show strange tricks which you call signs of faith."

In this special difficulty men are often disappointed because the Bible does not directly help. Dr. McFadyen clearly states the truth of the matter—"Just as the Bible assumes the existence of God, so it also assumes the naturalness of prayer. It does not answer, and, for the most part does not even raise the problems which bear so heavily upon educated men today." In the Bible there is no difficulty in the way of fleece on the same night becoming both wet and dry (Judges 6:37ff); the sun may stop or proceed (Josh. 10:13), the shadow on the sun dial go forwards or backwards (Isaiah 38:8); the axe head may sink or float (II Kings 6:5ff); and the prison doors may open without human help (Acts 5:19). *Like all people of the generations during which the Bible was being written, the writers of Scripture for the most part described events in terms of miracle and not of law.*

But this biblical assumption that prayer is entirely natural, and this description of the results of prayer in terms of miracle, rather increase than allay the perplexity of many Christians. "This world of the Bible is not our world," they cry in doubt. "Show us a single place in the world in which *we* live, where we cannot depend for certain on nature's regularity. We predict sunrise and sunset to the second and they never fail. We plot the course of the planets and they are never late. The achievements of our modern world rest on the discovery that we can rely on the same things happening under the same conditions, always and everywhere. When we figure strain on a bridge we know that the laws of mechanics will not shift over-night. Indeed, the marvel of our present age is symbolized by the English astronomers, going out to Africa to study an eclipse, and standing at last on the veldt beside their instruments. 'Now,' said one, watch in hand, 'if we have made no mistake in our calculations, the eclipse should begin at once.' On the instant the shadow of the moon pushed its edge over the rim of the sun! What is the use of praying in a world like that?—'Stern as fate, absolute as tyranny, merciless as death; too vast to praise, too inexorable to propitiate; it has no ear for prayer, no heart for sympathy, no arm to save.' "

No one needs to travel far to discover men whose religious think-ing has stumbled over this difficulty. It is, therefore, important thus early in our discussion to see clearly that *natural law is not at all what superficial thinking makes it appear to be.* Dealing with the reign of law is like going through the Simplon tunnel. Go a little way and one has darkness and imprisonment. Go a little further and one has light, liberty, and the far stretches of the Italian hills. The classic word of Bacon is nowhere more true than here—"This I dare affirm in knowledge of nature that a little natural philosophy, and the first entrance into it, doth dispose the opinion to atheism, but on the other side, much natural philosophy and wading deep into it, will bring about men's minds to religion."

II

We may approach this deeper truth about "natural philosophy" by remarking that the man who believes in nature's inexorable regu-larity immune from personal control, ought not to expect, under ordinary circumstances, to see water flow up hill. As a matter of fact, however, he can see it any day. Reservoirs are built among the mountains or pumping stations are established and water runs up hill and down dale with equal facility and seeks the topmost stories of the tallest buildings. And this is the important secret there re-vealed—*Persons cannot violate the law of gravitation, but they can use the law-abiding force of gravitation to do what, without their cooperation, never would occur.*

So ordinarily a heavy substance will not float upon a lighter one. But every day iron steamships plow the sea, and heavier-than-air machines navigate the sky. Here too is revealed the fact that persons while they can never break nor change laws, can utilize, manipulate, and combine the forces which laws control to do what those forces by themselves would not accomplish. The insight which takes from the heart of religion all fear of the reign of law is this: *Personality, even in ourselves, how much more in God, is the master and not merely the slave of all law-abiding forces.* As Huxley put it, "The organized and highly developed sciences and arts of the present day have endowed man with a command over the course of non-human nature greater than that once attributed to the magicians."

This truth underlies all our modern material accomplishments. If an engineer proposed to bridge a stream, who would say to him: "It is impossible. The laws of nature forbid hanging iron over air"? He could answer: "I am not merely the slave of nature but in part its master. Nature can be *used* as well *as obeyed*." And if one insisted to the contrary, claiming that natural laws are inviolable, the engineer's reply is evident: "The inviolability of natural laws is the beauty of them. They are trusty servants. They can be depended on. They are unwavering yesterday, today, and forever. And if you will watch, you will see me say to this force, come, and it will come; to this force, go, and it will go; and I, a person, will manipulate and utilize the law-abiding energies of nature, making infinitely varied combinations of invariable procedures, until millions of men shall cross this river on my bridge."

III

So important is it clearly to see the truth that personality, even in ourselves, can work the most unexpected results, not by violating laws, but by using knowledge of them, that we may well approach it from another angle. When men are dismayed by the inflexibility of law, they are thinking of cause and effect as forming a rigid system in whose established order no break can come. Now, we may not enter here into the philosophy of causation, but it is worth noting that in practical experience we seem to be dealing with *two kinds of cause*. When the atmospheric pressure makes the wind blow that is one sort; when a man sails by that same wind, skilfully tacking until he reaches his destination, that is another. In one case we have absolutely predetermined procedure; in the other we have a personal will serving a personal purpose by utilizing the predetermined procedure. These two kinds of cause seem everywhere to be at work. When the snow falls on the walk, its removal may be effected by *natural causes,* the sunshine or the rain. But its removal may also be effected by *personal causes.* A man with an ideal and a shovel may put his shovel at the service of his ideal and clear the walk. Personal causation is everywhere in evidence and when the reign of cause and effect seems rigid and merciless, it is because we forget how pliable law-abiding forces are in the hands of personality.[1]

Strange that we should forget it! All our human achievements are illustrations of this truth. Natural causes cannot explain St. Paul's Cathedral. Gravitation never cried to his brethren, the forces of nature, "Come, let us conspire to build a temple to God." The cause of St. Paul's Cathedral is personality utilizing its knowledge of laws. Natural causation cannot explain the sonatas of Beethoven. Nothing could be more mathematically exact than the laws of sound-vibration, but all great music bears witness to the power of personality when it uses its privilege of manipulating law-abiding sounds. Natural causation may explain the straits of Gibraltar but it cannot explain the Panama Canal. Personal cause alone can account for that.

> "A man went down to Panama
>   Where many a man had died,
> To slit the sliding mountains
>   And lift the eternal tide.
> A man stood up in Panama,
>   And the mountains stood aside."

One of the most liberating conceptions that can come to any mind is this perception that *law-abiding forces can be made the servants of personal will.* The only possibility of denying this truth lies in a theory of absolute determinism that makes the whole world a material machine with personality a helpless cog in the wheels. Grant, even in the least degree, what experience asserts and the greatest philosophies confirm, the truth of individual initiative; and we have a new element in the reign of cause and effect—namely personal causation. *Continually we are projecting personal cause into the realm of natural causes.* And when one deeply considers this, he sees what we call natural cause may not be *impersonal* cause at all, *that our limited control of universal forces may be a counterpart*

---

[1]One of the best philosophic statements of this truth will be found in Prof. G. H. Palmer's "The Problem of Freedom."

of God's unlimited control. Then all cause would be personal, and all procedure that we call natural would be God's regular ways of acting. Neither with God nor man do cause and effect make an iron system in which personality is enslaved. Rather they present to personality a reliable instrument through which personal freedom is continually expressed.

IV

Many of the arguments against prayer, based on the reign of law, bear with exactly the same force against any request made of an earthly friend. God cannot answer prayer because he cannot interfere with the reign of law? Let us see! A child falls from an open window and, badly hurt, calls to his father. Will the father regret his inability to help because the reign of law prevents? On the contrary, the father will set about using his knowledge of the reign of law as speedily as possible. He lifts the child from the ground although gravitation by itself would have kept the child there. He calls up the hospital by telephone and in that act uses a combination of natural forces, put together by personal will, so wonderful that the thought of it may well make even a modern man gasp. The ambulance clangs down the street, representing a utilization of nature where knowledge of hundreds of invariable mechanical, physical, and chemical laws has been utilized. The surgeon projects personal will against the dead set and certainly fatal outcome of natural causation, and the child is saved. *How many laws did that father violate? Not one, but he utilized knowledge of so many that no man can count them, and he employed that knowledge as the instrument of his love in the service of his child.*

Whether, therefore, we consider the ways in which men subject natural processes to their will; or the ways in which personal cause controls natural causes; or the ways in which we answer requests, not by violating laws but by using our knowledge of them, we come to the same conclusion: personality can control the universal forces to serve personal ends. Scientific laws are human statements and increasingly true statements of nature's invariable procedures, but the procedures are always pliable in the hands of human intelligence and will. *Do we mean to say that God is less free than we are? Are we, the creatures, in so large measure masters of law-abiding forces and is he, the Creator, a slave to them? Are the universal powers*

*plastic and usable in our hands, and in his hands stiff and rigid?
The whole analogy of human experience suggests that the world is
not governed by law; that it is governed by God according to law.
He providentially utilizes, manipulates, and combines his own invariable ways of acting to serve his own eternal purposes.*

v

Our fundamental fallacy about God is our thought of him as an
artificer, now far-off, who has left this machine of his running by
its own laws, and who cannot do anything with it except by intervention. Let us banish so primitive a picture of God, so childish
a conception of the universe! He is not far-off. He is the Indwelling
Presence in the World, as our life is in our bodies, controlling all.
He is the immanent and eternal Creator, and the laws, some known
to us, some unknown, are his ways of doing things. He is not a
prisoner caught in the mechanism of his own world; he is not reduced to the impotency of Louis Philippe, "I reign, but I do not
govern." He is free, more free than we can guess, to use the forces
he has ordained. *Providence is possible.* A youth can deflect a brook's
course from one channel to another. God can do with any life and
with the course of history, what we do with a brook. The laws are
all in his leash. Says Jesus, "Not a sparrow shall fall on the ground
without your Father" (Matt. 10:29).

While the Bible, therefore, does not deal with the modern problem of natural law, in its reference to prayer, we still may share
with the Bible that utter confidence in the power and willingness
and liberty of God to help his children, which makes the Scriptures
radiant with trust and hope. When the Bible says, "God hath spoken
once, twice have I heard this, that power belongeth unto God"
(Psalm 62:11); or "Jehovah is my strength and my shield; my heart
hath trusted in him, and I am helped" (Psalm 28:7); or "To them
that love God all things work together for good" (Rom. 8:28)—it
is saying nothing that the most thorough believer in the reign of
law may not say too. There are many prayers that God *must not*
answer, but there are no good prayers which God *cannot* answer.
He is the master of all laws, known to us and unknown. When God
utilizes his knowledge of his own laws, who can say in advance what
may happen? God is free, so far as the mere possibilities are concerned, to answer any petition whatsoever; and if a prayer is left

unanswered it is not because the reign of law prevents. *It is because there are vast realms where God must not substitute our wish for his plan.*

This last statement deserves emphasis. We may prefer to have the sun rise earlier, or to have a dozen colors in the spectrum, or to think without association of ideas, or to sin and not suffer; but we may as well spare our pains. *God does not remake his world for the asking, not because he cannot, but because he must not.* It may be convenient for us to substitute rain for sunshine or sunshine for rain, but we are likely to be vainly substituting presumption for faith when we try to control the weather. As the old rabbis put it: A mother had two sons, one a gardener and the other a potter. Said the gardener, "O mother, pray God for rain to water my plants." Said the potter, "O mother, pray God for sunshine to dry my pots." Now the mother loved them equally well. Shall she pray for rain or sun? Nay, she would best leave it in the hands of God.

When entire confidence has been established, therefore, in the power and liberty of God to utilize any force at any time, a due humility will restrain us from making a presumptuous application of this truth to prayer. Within the realm of personal relationships the effect of prayer is so clear that our faith in prayer's efficacy has assured ground in experience, but the power of prayer to affect the objective processes of nature is incapable of scientific demonstration. We never can so completely isolate an event, like a change in the weather, as to prove that nothing but our prayer could have caused it. To be sure no man can draw a clear boundary, saying, "Within this we may expect God to use his laws in answer to our prayers, and without we may look for nothing of the kind." Professor Browne's word is sane and helpful: *"To pray about everything, in submission to God's will, would be both more human and more Christian than a scrupulous limitation of our prayers to what we might think permissible subjects of petition."*

But it must be obvious that we should never presumptuously demand the use of natural forces in the objective world to serve our personal purpose, and then confidently expect our prayer to work the change. Before sun and rain, as Jesus said, the just and unjust seem to fare alike (Matt. 5:45). Lyman Beecher's public claim that

the burning of an unorthodox church was due to the special judgment of God on false doctrine was shown to be perilous, as well as
untrue, when the next week Lyman Beecher's church burned down.
The forces of the external world are in the hands of God to do with
them as he wishes, but that does not necessarily mean that he must
do with them as we wish. God must not surrender his sovereignty
on demand. It is far better that man should learn the discipline of
law than be exempt for the asking. Prayer distinctly is *not* "a machine warranted by the theologians to make God do what his clients
want!"

In all our praying therefore, we need to remember the distinction, to use Trumbull's phrases, between *"faith in prayer"* and
"prayer in faith." Faith in prayer may be presumptuous and clamorous; it may present ultimatums to the Almighty demanding his
acquiescence; it may try to make of prayer a magic demand on
God. But prayer in faith asks everything in entire submission to
the will of God. It desires never to force its wish on the Eternal
Purpose but always to align its wish with the Eternal Purpose. It
pleads passionately for its needs; but it closes its petition, as the
Master did, "Thy will be done." Prayer in faith rejoices in God's
sovereignty, is confident that all forces are in his leash, and that
to those who love him all things work together for good. Prayer thus
becomes meaningful because God is free to do what he will in his
world; but prayer does not on that account become presumptuous
as though God must do what *we* will in his world.

VII

There is a realm, however, where none need be hesitant in expecting answer to prayer. *Prayer is the law of personal relationships.*
It is important to see clearly that all laws do not apply in all realms.
Gravitation for example is not universal; it obtains without exception in the objective physical world, but it does not range up into
the personal, spiritual world. We come there into a new realm where
we deal with realities that cannot be caught in test-tubes, measured
by yardsticks, or weighed in scales. In that new realm new laws are
at work. Gravitation cannot break up into the world of spirit, although spirit can break down and use the force of gravitation. Laws
are thus arranged in regimes. When one leaves the inorganic world
for the organic, he leaves behind him laws that are now no longer

applicable; when he leaves the world of plants for the world of men, he moves up to laws that do not concern plants but do apply to men; and in this higher realm where men deal with one another and with God, there are conditions of communion, laws of fellowship and prayer. One cannot imagine Jesus asking for an objective change in the physical world, without entire willingness to submit to a negative answer; but when he goes up into the mountain alone to commune with God, he goes with absolute assurance that the strength and peace and vision which he needs will come. Personal relationship is the unique realm of prayer. As one reads the great prayers of the church he sees that in this realm supremely the people of God have prayed with confidence, have expected answer and have not been disappointed.

> "Lord, what a change within us one short hour
>   Spent in Thy presence will avail to make!
>   What heavy burdens from our bosoms take;
> What parched grounds refresh, as with a shower!
> We kneel, and all around us seems to lower;
>   We rise, and all the distant and the near
>   Stands forth in sunny outline, brave and clear!
> We kneel, how weak! we rise, how full of power!
> Why, therefore, should we do ourselves this wrong,
> Or others, that we are not always strong;
> That we are ever overborne with care;
>   That we should ever weak or heartless be,
> Anxious or troubled, when with us is prayer,
>   And joy and strength and courage are with Thee?"

SUGGESTIONS FOR THOUGHT AND DISCUSSION

If things are going to happen in any case according to fixed law, what is the use of petitioning for change?

What effect does knowledge of the reign of law have upon a man's attitude toward prayer?

How far can personal volition control the operation of natural forces?

What is the difference between violating a natural law and using a law-abiding force to accomplish something which would not have happened in the ordinary course of nature?

How far is the injection of a personal will into the operation of natural laws a violation of such laws?

To what degree is the Psalmist's faith in the controlling presence of God in his world justified?

How far could parents meet the need of their children if they were bound rigidly by the reign of law?

To what extent is doubt about the possibility of answer to prayer due to the belief that it violates law, and to what extent to lack of understanding of the operation of law?

How far is confidence in God's control of natural forces inconsistent with a belief in the reliability of law?

To what extent does the reign of law prevent the answer to prayer?

Are there any prayers which God cannot answer?

How far is the Bible's confidence in the power and willingness and liberty of God to help his children justified?

How do you think God's plans for the world affect his response to individual prayers?

What is the difference between law in the realm of nature and law in the personal, spiritual world?

What is the difference between faith in prayer and prayer in faith?

CHAPTER VII

Unanswered Prayer

DAILY READINGS

First Day, Seventh Week

Complaint about unanswered prayer is nothing new. Consider this cry of distress with which Habakkuk opens his book:

The burden which Habakkuk the prophet did see. O Jehovah, how long shall I cry, and thou wilt not hear? I cry out unto thee of violence, and thou wilt not save. Why dost thou show me iniquity, and look upon perverseness? for destruction and violence are before me; and there is strife, and contention riseth up. Therefore the law is slacked, and justice doth never go forth; for the wicked doth compass about the righteous; therefore justice goeth forth perverted. . . . Thou that art of purer eyes than to behold evil, and that canst not look on perverseness, wherefore lookest thou upon them that deal treacherously, and holdest thy peace when the wicked swalloweth up the man that is more righteous than he?—Habakkuk 1:1-4, 13.

The weekly comment will take up the reasons for such an experience as is revealed here, but in the daily readings let us consider the *unreasonableness of allowing such experiences to cause the abandoning of prayer.* For one thing, unanswered petition ought not to cause the abandonment of all praying because much of the greatest praying is not petition at all. Even the pagans in their polytheism have occasionally perceived this truth; as, for example, in an ancient book, De Mysteriis Aegyptorum, "Prayer is not a means of inducing the gods to change the course of things, but their own gift of communion with themselves, the blessing of the living gods upon their children." When one turns to Christian experience he finds this aspect of prayer everywhere magnified and exalted. When Tennyson described prayer's meaning for his life he said, "Prayer is like opening a sluice between the great ocean and our little channels, when the sea gathers itself together and flows in at full tide." Consider how entirely this realm of prayer lies outside the disappointments of denied petition for changed circumstances.

Father, I thank Thee for Thy mercies which are new every morning. For the gift of sleep; for health and strength; for the vision of another day with its fresh opportunities of work and service; for all these and more than these, I thank Thee. Before looking on the face of men I would look on Thee, who art the health of my countenance and my God. Not without Thy guidance would I go forth to meet the duties and tasks of the day. Strengthen me so that in all my work I may be faithful; amid trials, courageous; in suffering, patient; under disappointment, full of hope in Thee. Grant this for Thy goodness' sake. Amen.—Samuel McComb.

Second Day, Seventh Week

How precious also are thy thoughts unto me, O God!
How great is the sum of them!
If I should count them, they are more in number than the sand:
When I awake, I am still with thee. . . .
Search me, O God, and know my heart:
Try me, and know my thoughts;
And see if there be any wicked way in me,
And lead me in the way everlasting.
                    —Psalm 139:17, 18, 23, 24.

Consider the Psalmist's use of prayer as an opening of the heart to God's search, a means of restandardizing the life and aligning it continually with God's will. Should any number of disappointed petitions for external things blind our eyes to this transforming use of prayer? A typical result of Quintin Hogg's work for boys in London was seen in Jem Nicholls, a reclaimed lad of the streets. When Jem was asked, after Mr. Hogg's death, how the fight for character was coming on, he said, "I have a bit of trouble in keeping straight, but I thank God all is well. You see, I carry a photo of 'Q. H.' with me always, and whenever I am tempted, I take it out and his look is a wonderful help, and by the grace of God I am able to overcome all." Prayer can be in our lives this sort of cleansing and empowering look at our Lord. It sets us right, reestablishes our standards, confirms our best resolves. After all, is not this what we most want prayer for? Are we not showing poor judgment when we surrender this kind of praying because other kinds do not always seem effective?

Almighty God, who by Thy grace and providence hast brought my great and crying sins to light, I most humbly beseech Thee to continue Thy grace and mercy to me, that my conscience being now awakened, I may call my ways to remembrance, and confess, and bewail and abhor all the sins of my life past. And, O merciful God, give me true repentance for them, even that repentance to which Thou hast promised mercy and pardon, that even the consequences of my wrongdoing may bring a blessing to me, and that in all I may find mercy at Thy hands, through the merits and mediation of our Lord Jesus Christ. Amen.—Bishop Thos. Wilson (1663-1755).

Third Day, Seventh Week

Seek ye Jehovah while he may be found; call ye upon him while he is near: let the wicked forsake his way, and the unrighteous man his thoughts; and let him return unto Jehovah, and he will have mercy upon him; and to our God, for he will abundantly pardon. For my thoughts are not your thoughts, neither are your ways my ways, saith Jehovah. For as the heavens are higher than the earth, so are my ways higher than your ways, and my thoughts than your thoughts. For as the rain cometh down and the snow from heaven, and returneth not thither, but watereth the earth, and maketh it bring forth and bud, and giveth seed to the sower and bread to the eater; so shall my word be that goeth forth out of my mouth: it shall not return unto me void, but it shall accomplish that which I please, and it shall prosper in the thing whereto I sent it.—Isaiah 55:6-11.

To make unanswered petition an excuse for abandoning all prayer is clearly unreasonable when we stop to consider how utterly unfitted we are to substitute our wish for God's will, and what appalling results would follow if all our requests were answered. Think over the faith in God's providence, superior wisdom, and mercy which Isaiah here makes the basis of prayer. Is it not clear that our clamorous demands that this kind of God should *please us,* justify Longfellow in his table-talk in breaking out into this indignant and somewhat exaggerated reproof: "What discord should we bring into the universe if our prayers were all answered! Then *we* should govern the world and not God. And do you think we should govern it better? It gives me only pain when I hear the long, wearisome petitions of men asking for they know not what. As frightened women clutch at the reins when there is danger, so do we grasp at God's government with our prayers. Thanksgiving with a full heart—and the rest silence and submission to the divine will!"

Thou hast called us to Thyself, most merciful Father, with love and with promises abundant; and we are witnesses that it is not in vain that we drew near to Thee. We bear witness to Thy faithfulness. Thy promises are Yea and Amen. Thy blessings are exceeding abundant more than we know or think. We thank Thee for the privilege of prayer, and for Thine answers to prayer; and we rejoice that Thou dost not answer according to our petitions. We are blind, and are constantly seeking things which are not best for us. If Thou didst grant all our desires according to our requests, we should be ruined. In dealing with our little children we give them, not the things which they ask for, but the things which we judge to be best for them; and Thou, our Father, art by Thy providence overruling our ignorance and our headlong mistakes, and are doing for us, not so much the things that we request of Thee as the things that we should ask; and we are, day by day, saved from peril and from ruin by Thy better knowledge and by Thy careful love. Amen.—Henry Ward Beecher.

Fourth Day, Seventh Week

Yet a further reason for the way we let denied petition break our faith in prayer is that we fail to see how often God answers our prayers in ways that we do not expect and, it may be, do not like. Consider Paul's experience, in the one petition that, so far as we have record, he ever offered for his own individual need:

And by reason of the exceeding greatness of the revelations, that I should not be exalted overmuch, there was given to me a thorn in the flesh, a messenger of Satan to buffet me, that I should not be exalted overmuch. Concerning this thing I besought the Lord thrice, that it might depart from me. And he hath said unto me, My grace is sufficient for thee: for my power is made perfect in weakness. Most gladly therefore will I rather glory in my weaknesses, that the power of Christ may rest upon me.—II Cor. 12:7-9.

How often do God's replies thus come to us in disguise, so that we, lacking Paul's insight, do not recognize them. Henry Ward Beecher stated with characteristic humor what is often a very serious truth in the practice of prayer. "A woman," he said, "prays for patience and God sends her a green cook." That is, we seek for a *thing*, and God gives us a *chance*. When our answers come so, they are likely neither to be recognized nor welcomed. The old Olney Hymns contain two stanzas that are applicable to not a little experience with prayer:

> "I asked the Lord that I might grow,
>   In faith, and love and ev'ry grace,
> Might more of his salvation know,
>   And seek more earnestly his face.

> "Twas he who taught me thus to pray,
>   And he I know has answered prayer,
> But it has been in such a way
>   As almost drove me to despair."

O God, forgive the poverty, the pettiness, Lord, the childish folly of our prayers. Listen, not to our words, but to the groanings that cannot be uttered; hearken, not to our petitions, but to the crying of our need. So often we pray for that which is already ours, neglected and unappropriated; so often for that which never can be ours; so often for that which we must win ourselves; and then labour endlessly for that which can only come to us in prayer.

How often we have prayed for the coming of Thy kingdom, yet when it has sought to come through us we have sometimes barred the way; we have wanted it without in others, but not in our own hearts. We feel it is we who stand between man's need and Thee; between ourselves and what we might be; and we have no trust in our own strength, or loyalty, or courage.

O give us to love Thy will, and seek Thy kingdom first of all.
Sweep away our fears, our compromise, our weakness, lest at last
we be found fighting against Thee. Amen.—W. E. Orchard.

Fifth Day, Seventh Week

But if any of you lacketh wisdom, let him ask of God, who giveth
to all liberally and upbraideth not; and it shall be given him. But
let him ask in faith, nothing doubting: for he that doubteth is like
the surge of the sea driven by the wind and tossed. For let not that
man think that he shall receive anything of the Lord; a double-
minded man, unstable in all his ways.—James 1:5-8.

Our petitions seem to us to be denied and we give up praying in
discouragement, when the fact may be that God is suggesting to
us all the time ways in which we could answer our own requests.
Many a man asks for a *thing,* and God's answer is *wisdom sufficient*
to get the thing. Dean Bosworth puts it clearly: "Almost all the
petitions a disciple ever has occasion to make to his Father can be
answered without recourse to the so-called laws of nature, *if God*
has power to put a thought into the mind of man. Suppose that the
disciple wants work or money. If his Father has power to put an
appropriate suggestion into his mind, or into some other man's mind,
or into the minds of both, the prayer can be answered. And this
can be done by means of, and not in spite of, the laws of mental
action. We are able to put thoughts into each other's minds by means
of words, and science seems to be surely demonstrating the fact that
there are other ways of doing it. Jesus simply assumes that God has
so made the human mind that it is capable of an interchange of
thought with himself, its Heavenly Father."

O Thou, who art the true Sun of the world, ever rising, and never
going down; who, by Thy most wholesome appearing and sight dost
nourish, and gladden all things, in heaven and earth; we beseech
Thee mercifully to shine into our hearts, that the night and darkness
of sin, and the mists of error on every side, being driven away, by
the brightness of Thy shining within our hearts, we may all our life
walk without stumbling, as in the day-time, and, being pure and
clean from the works of darkness, may abound in all good works
which Thou hast prepared for us to walk in. Amen.—Erasmus
(1467-1536).

Sixth Day, Seventh Week

And he spake a parable unto them to the end that they ought always to pray, and not to faint; saying, There was in a city a judge, who feared not God, and regarded not man: and there was a widow in that city; and she came oft unto him, saying, Avenge me of mine adversary. And he would not for a while: but afterward he said within himself, Though I fear not God, nor regard man; yet because this widow troubleth me, I will avenge her, lest she wear me out by her continual coming. And the Lord said, Hear what the unrighteous judge saith. And shall not God avenge his elect, that cry to him day and night, and yet he is longsuffering over them? I say unto you, that he will avenge them speedily. Nevertheless, when the Son of man cometh, shall he find faith on the earth?—Luke 18:1-8.

Men often call their petitions unanswered because in their impatience they do not give God time. Remember that in this parable the judge stands *in contrast* with God, not in simi'arity with him, and that the lesson is: If it was worth while waiting persistently upon the unjust judge, how much more surely worth while to wait patiently on the fatherly God! Many of our greatest desires demand time, patience, persistent search, long waiting as conditions of their fulfillment. Our petitions sometimes are unanswered only because we too soon give them up as unanswered. Spurgeon put the case strongly: "It may be your prayer is like a ship, which, when it goes on a very long voyage, does not come home laden so soon; but when it does come home, it has a richer freight. Mere 'coasters' will bring you coals, or such like ordinary things; but they that go afar to Tarshish return with gold and ivory. Coasting prayers, such as we pray every day, bring us many necessaries, but there are great prayers, which, like the old Spanish galleons, cross the main ocean, and are longer out of sight, but come home deep laden with a golden freight."

O Merciful God, fill our hearts, we pray Thee, with the graces of Thy Holy Spirit, with love, joy, peace, long-suffering, gentleness, goodness, faith, meekness, temperance. Teach us to love those who hate us; to pray for those who despitefully use us; that we may be the children of Thee, our Father, who makest Thy sun to shine on

the evil and on the good, and sendest rain on the just and on the
unjust.—Anselm (1033-1109).

Seventh Day, Seventh Week

Beloved, think it not strange concerning the fiery trial among
you, which cometh upon you to prove you, as though a strange
thing happened unto you: but insomuch as ye are partakers of
Christ's sufferings, rejoice; that at the revelation of his glory also
ye may rejoice with exceeding great joy. If ye are reproached for
the name of Christ, blessed are ye; because the Spirit of glory and
the Spirit of God resteth upon you. For let none of you suffer as a
murderer, or a thief, or an evildoer, or as a meddler in other men's
matters: but if a man suffer as a Christian, let him not be ashamed;
but let him glorify God in this name. . . . Wherefore let them also
that suffer according to the will of God commit their souls in well-
doing unto a faithful Creator.—I Peter 4:12-16, 19.

Note the serious situation reflected in this Scripture, the suffering
endured, the "fiery trial" to be faced, and consider the spirit of
prayer in the last verse, where "as to a faithful Creator" they commit their souls. Some people make an unreasonable surrender of
their praying, because they have been disappointed in getting their
desires, and suppose that the great pray-ers have estimated the value
of prayer in terms of the trouble out of which it saved them. On the
contrary, many a saint has prayed his best for changed circumstances
and then has committed his soul "as to a faithful Creator," although
the outward trouble still was there. "Chinese" Gordon was a great
believer in prayer; he said that he "prayed his boats up the Nile";
but he also has left on record this statement: "I think all prayer for
temporalities must be made in subjection to God's will, with this
reservation—if it falls in with his great scheme. The person who
prays must be ready to have his request denied, if it runs counter to
God's rule, which is dictated by infinite wisdom."

O Father, who hast ordained that we be set within a scheme of
circumstance, and that in stern conflict we should find our strength
and triumph over all; withhold not from us the courage by which
alone we can conquer. Still our tongues of their weak complainings,
steel our hearts against all fear, and in joyfully accepting the condi-

tions of our earthly pilgrimage may we come to possess our souls and achieve our purposed destiny.

It has pleased Thee to hide from us a perfect knowledge, yet Thou callest for a perfect trust in Thee. We cannot see to-morrow, we know not the way that we take, darkness hangs about our path and mystery meets us at every turn. Yet Thou hast shut us up to final faith in goodness, justice, truth; that loving these for themselves alone, we may find the love that passeth knowledge, and look upon Thy face.

O suffer us not for any terror of darkness or from any torment of mind to sin against our souls, or to fail at last of Thee. Amen.— W. E. Orchard.

COMMENT FOR THE WEEK

I

To a beginner in the high art of praying the Bible is often a very disheartening book. Its characters appear at first sight to enjoy the uninterrupted experience of answered prayer. The refrain of the Psalmist seems typical: "Thou hast given him his heart's desire, thou hast not withholden the request of his lips" (Psalm 21:2). If the Bible, however, knew no other experience with prayer than the enjoyment of successful petition, it would be a book utterly inadequate to meet our needs. One of the sorest trials of our faith is petition unanswered. It is worth our notice, therefore, that the Bible itself records the experience of ungranted prayer. Even in the Psalms one finds not alone jubilant gratitude over petitions won but despondent sorrow over petitions denied. "O my God, I cry in the day-time, but thou answerest not; and in the night season, and am not silent" (Psalm 22:2).

Indeed, upon examination, the Bible turns out to be full of unanswered prayers. Moses prays to enter the Promised Land, but dies on Nebo's top, his request refused. In the midst of national calamity the patriot lifts his Lamentation, "Thou hast covered thyself with a cloud, so that no prayer can pass through" (Lam. 3:44); and the prophet Habakkuk in his despondency exclaims, "O Jehovah, how long shall I cry, and thou wilt not hear?" (Hab. 1:2). Paul prays thrice that a vexatious, physical handicap, a "thorn in the flesh," which hinders his missionary labors, may be removed; but for the rest of his life he is compelled to make the best of it and to let it make the best of him (II Cor. 12:9). Even the Master in the Garden prays for release from the appalling cup, but goes out to drink it to the dregs.

Not only do we meet in the Scriptures such outstanding examples of unanswered prayer; we find as well whole classes of men whose petitions are on principle denied. In the first chapter of Isaiah men are praying and God is speaking to them, "When ye make many prayers, I will not hear: your hands are full of blood" (Isaiah 1:15). In the fourth chapter of James' Epistle men are praying, and the Apostle says, "Ye ask, and receive not, because ye ask amiss, that ye may spend it in your pleasures" (James 4:3). Throughout the Old Testament the reader runs continually on verses such as these: "What is the hope of the godless? . . . Will God hear *his* cry?" (Job 27:8, 9); "Pray not thou for this people, neither lift up a cry or prayer for them; for I will not hear them in the time that they cry unto me" (Jer. 11:14); "If I regard iniquity in my heart, the Lord will not hear me" (Psalm 66:18). Even in the Gospels, Jesus, the supreme believer in prayer, tells his disciples that if a man does not forgive his enemies, even his own prayer for God's pardon will be disregarded (Matt. 6:15). *The Bible is full of unanswered prayer.* We have here no monotonous, unreal record of petitions always granted. This book is no stranger to that complaint which, more than any puzzle over theory, makes confident prayer difficult: "I cry unto thee, and thou dost not answer me: I stand up, and thou gazest at me" (Job 30:20).

II

In dealing with this problem we should emphasize the truth before maintained that petition is by no means the only form of prayer. Even though a man never asked God for anything, he still could pray. Indeed, the value of prayer is made to hinge too often upon the granting of minor material requests. God is reduced to the office of a village charity organization doling out small supplies to improvident applicants. This conception of prayer's use and value is infinitely removed from the elevated thought of Scripture. When we listen there in the places where men pray, we hear, for example: "Bless Jehovah, O my soul; and all that is within me, bless his holy name" (Psalm 103:1). It is the prayer of *adoration.* Or we hear the

cry of a great statesman, remaking a ruined nation, "O my God, I
am ashamed and blush to lift up my face to thee, my God; for our
iniquities are increased over our head, and our guiltiness is grown up
unto the heavens" (Ezra 9:6). It is the prayer of *confession*. We
hear a grateful Psalmist pray: "I will extol thee, O Jehovah; for
thou hast raised me up . . . O Jehovah my God, I will give thanks
unto thee for ever" (Psalm 30:1, 12). It is the prayer of *thanksgiving*. We hear the vow: "Teach me, O Jehovah, the way of thy
statutes; and I shall keep it unto the end. Give me understanding,
and I shall keep thy law; yea, I shall observe it with my whole heart"
(Psalm 119:33, 34). It is the prayer of *consecration*. And often, a
voice like this is heard: "How precious also are thy thoughts unto
me, O God! How great is the sum of them! . . . When I awake, I
am still with thee" (Psalm 139:17, 18). It is the prayer of *communion*. Adoration, confession, thanksgiving, consecration, communion—these are the great prayers of the Book as they are of the
soul. *Petition is only one province in the vast Kingdom of Prayer.
Whatever our difficulties there, the wide ranges of prayer are not
closed to us.*

Nevertheless this province of petition is important. It is not the
whole of prayer, but it is the original form of prayer and never can
be nor ought to be outgrown. Men cannot be content simply to
praise God, confess to him, thank him, make vows of devotion, and
enjoy communion with him. Men have desires, all the way from the
long-sought coming of the Kingdom to the welfare of their loved
ones and the prosperity of their daily business, to whose furtherance
they instinctively call the help of any god in whom they really believe. "Thy will be done on earth as it is in heaven," and "Give us
this day our daily bread," are both petitions; and they belong in the
Lord's Prayer, together with "Hallowed be thy name." Petition, in
its lower forms, trying to make God a mere means to serve some
selfish, external end, is the result of ignorant, unspiritual immaturity.
But petitions that well up out of mankind's deep desires for real
good, are an integral part of prayer. They are to the whole domain
what the thirteen original states are to America; not the whole of it,
nor the major portion of it, but the primary nucleus of it and the
initial influence in it.

Moreover, the Bible, with all its emphasis upon the other aspects
of prayer, uses words very explicit, sweeping, and confident about
petition: "Call unto me, and I will answer thee" (Jer. 33:3); "Ask,

and it shall be given you" (Matt. 7:7); "All things, whatsoever ye shall ask in prayer, believing, ye shall receive" (Matt. 21:22); "All things whatsoever ye pray and ask for, believe that ye receive them, and ye shall have them" (Mark 11:24); "If two of you shall agree on earth as touching anything that they shall ask, it shall be done for them of my Father" (Matt. 18:19). What expectations such words awaken! And what a puzzling, baffling obstacle to active faith is the repeated denial of our requests! What is the use of proving that prayer *can* bring results if our experience shows that it *does* not?

III

One obvious reason for our unanswered petitions is, of course, *the ignorance of our asking*. Piety is no guarantee of wisdom. One has but to consider the spectacle of all sorts and conditions of men at prayer, voicing to God their various and often contradictory desires; praying vehemently on opposite sides of the same war; some even praying, like the Bourbon king, that they may be allowed to sin once more; and almost all of us praying in ignorance of our profoundest needs, to see that many petitions *must* be denied. Indeed, instead of calling prayers unanswered, it is far truer to recognize that "No" is as real an answer as "Yes," and often far more kind. When one considers the partialness of our knowledge, the narrowness of our outlook, our little skill in tracing the far-off consequences of our desire, he sees how often God must speak to us, as Jesus did to the ambitious woman, "Ye know not what ye ask" (Matt. 20:22). This suggestion is no special pleading, superficially to evade a difficulty. Rabindranath Tagore, the Bengali poet, was not constructing a Christian apologetic, but was stating a profound human experience, when he wrote:

"My desires are many and my cry is pitiful, but ever didst thou save me by hard refusals; and this strong mercy has been wrought into my life through and through."

This suggestion gains force when we perceive that often, *if God granted the form of our petition, he would deny the substance of our desire*. In one of the most impressive passages in his "Confessions," St. Augustine pictures his mother, Monica, praying all one night, in a sea-side chapel on the north African coast, that God would not let her son sail for Italy. She wanted Augustine to be a

Christian. She could not endure losing him from her influence. If under her care, he still was far from being Christ's, what would he be in Italy, home of licentiousness and splendor, of manifold and alluring temptations? And even while she prayed there passionately for her son's retention at home, he sailed, by the grace of God, for Italy, where, persuaded by Ambrose, he became a Christian in the very place from which his mother's prayers would have kept him. The form of her petition was denied; the substance of her desire was granted. As St. Augustine himself puts it: "Thou, in the depth of thy counsels, hearing the main point of her desire, regardedst not what she *then asked*, that thou mightest make me what she *ever desired*." It would be a sorry world for all of us, if our unwise petitions did not often have "No" for their answer.

IV

Another plain reason for our denied requests is that *we continually try to make prayer a substitute for intelligence and work.* We have already seen that there are three chief ways in which men cooperate with God: thinking, working, and praying. *Now, no one of these three can ever take the place of another.* Each has its peculiar realm. No human mind may be acute and penetrating enough exactly to trace the boundaries, but it is clear that the boundaries must be there. When our petitions cross over into the realms where results must be achieved, not by asking, but by working and thinking, the petitions cannot be granted.

There are prayers, for example, which attempt to achieve by supplication what can be achieved only by effective *thinking.* Consider what this world would become if everything could be accomplished by prayer. What if men could sail their ships as well by prayer alone as by knowledge of the science of navigation; could swing their bridges as firmly by petition only as by studying engineering laws; could light their houses, send their messages, and work out their philosophies by mere entreaty? Is it not clear that if, as in fairytales, we had the power of omnipotent wishing conferred upon us, we never would use our intelligence at all? If life is to mean development and discipline, some things must be impossible until men think, no matter how hard men pray. If a boy asks his father to work out his arithmetic lesson because he wishes to play, will the father do it? The father loves the boy; he could work out the lesson, but he must not. The boy's prayer must never be made a substitute for his intellectual discipline. The father, in answer to the boy's request, may encourage him, assist him, stand by him and see him through; but the father must not do for the boy anything that the boy can possibly do for himself. Harsh though at times it may seem, God surely must require us as individuals and as a race to endure the discipline of painful enterprise and struggle, rather than find an easy relief by asking.

There are prayers, also, which attempt to accomplish by supplication what can be accomplished only by *work*. In one of the most dramatic scenes of the Exodus, where the Israelites are caught with the unfordable Red Sea in front and the pursuing Egyptians behind, Moses goes apart to pray. The reply which he receives from Jehovah is startling. It is nothing less than a rebuke for having prayed: "Wherefore criest thou unto me? speak unto the children of Israel, that they go forward" (Ex. 14:15). It is as though God were saying, "I have everything prepared for your aggressive action. I have done the last thing that I can do, until you resolutely take advantage of it. It is your move! You cannot obtain by prayer what comes only as the reward of work." Such a rebuke many of our prayers deserve. We forget the proverb: "If wishes were horses, beggars would ride."

When one studies the great servants of the Kingdom at prayer, he always finds in them this sturdy common-sense. If ever an enterprise was begun, continued, and ended in prayer, it was Nehemiah's reconstruction of the Hebrew commonwealth; but Nehemiah always *combined* prayer and work, without *confusing* them: "I prayed unto the God of heaven. *And* I said unto the king" (Neh. 2:4, 5); "We made our prayer unto our God, *and* set a watch against them day and night" (Neh. 4:9); "Remember the Lord . . . *and* fight" (Neh. 4:14). So Cromwell prayed, but when he faced a weak and flaccid piety that made prayer a substitute for practical devotion, he put his feeling into a phrase as hard as his bullets: "Trust God and keep your powder dry." Such men have understood that God has *three* ways of accomplishing his will through men, not *one* way only. "Pray to God," said Spurgeon, "but keep the hammer going."

v

Still another reason for ungranted petition may be noted: *we are not ready for the reception of the gift which we desire.* The trouble is not with the petition but with us who offer it. We need not be wilfully wicked. We may simply lack that eager readiness to receive which voices itself in earnest, persistent prayer. The note of Jacob's wrestling with the angel, "I will not let thee go, except thou bless me" (Gen. 32:26), is lacking in our supplication. We are lacka-daisical in our desires and therefore are not importunate in our prayers.

At first it may be surprising, in view of all that has been said about the individual love of God, that we should insist on importunity in prayer. If God is good and wishes to give us the best, why must we clamor long after a real good, eagerly and patiently and with im-portunity seeking it?

At this point many of Jesus' sayings are difficult to understand. He clearly insisted on importunate prayer. "He spake a parable unto them to the end that they ought always to pray, and not to faint" (Luke 18:1), and the parable recorded a woman's tiresome, reiter-ated petitioning of a judge until he cried in despair, "I will avenge her, lest she wear me out by her continual coming." He who believed so fully in the utter willingness and power of God to help, even illustrated prayer by a man's arousal of a sleepy neighbor and his pestering persistence in calling for bread until "because of his im-portunity" he won his request (Luke 11:5f). We must allow for the picturesque exaggeration in these vivid parables; we must remember that they were supposed to illustrate only one aspect of prayer, not the whole of it; we must balance these passages by Jesus' own con-demnation of those who think they shall be "heard for their much speaking": but we must not thin out, until we lose it, the obvious meaning here. Jesus was insisting on tireless praying. He said prayer was seeking (Luke 11:9); and if one considers what intellectual search means, as when Copernicus questioned the heavens year after year to discover the truth, or what geographical search means, as when Peary tried undiscourageably for the Pole, he catches at least a faint idea of the Master's thought of prayer as an unwearied seeking after spiritual good. "For twenty-four years," said Peary, "sleeping or awake, to place the Stars and Stripes on the Pole had been my dream." That is the spirit of seeking, and that, the Master said, is the spirit of prayer.

The necessity of this sort of prayer is not difficult to understand. Boys on Hallowe'en ring bells and run. So, many of us pray. But any one who has serious business will wait for an answer to his summons and if need be, will ring again. The patient waiting, the reiterated demand are an expression and a test of our earnestness. When we said that both *"No"* and *"Yes"* were real answers to prayers, we did not exhaust the possibilities. There is another answer which God continually gives us—*"Wait."* For nearly two thousand years the church has been praying "that they may all be one." God never has said "No" to that, nor yet has he said "Yes." He has said "Wait." Since Jesus taught them first to pray, "Thy kingdom come," his disciples have lifted that supplication century after century; and "Lo! Thy church is praying yet, a thousand years the same." Great prayers such as these are not affairs of "Yes" or "No"; they reach over ages and bind together the aspirations of God's noblest sons; they are an eager, patient, persistent search after good.

Now compare with such undiscourageable prayers our individual spasms of petition. Our requests spurt up like intermittent geysers; we cry out and fall back again. We are not in earnest. "Easiness of desire," said Jeremy Taylor, "is a great enemy to the success of a good man's prayer. It must be an intent, zealous, busy, operative prayer. For consider what a huge indecency it is that a man should speak to God for a thing that he values not. Our prayers upbraid our spirits when we beg tamely for those things for which we ought to die." This, then, is the rationale of importunity in prayer, not that it is needed to coax God, but that it is needed alike to express and by expressing to deepen our eager readiness for the good we seek. *Some things God cannot give to a man until the man has prepared and proved his spirit by persistent prayer.* Such praying cleans the house, cleanses the windows, hangs the curtains, sets the table, opens the door, until God says, "Lo! The house is ready. Now may the guest come in."

VI

As we step, then, from the wider domain of prayer into the special province of petition, we can see three comprehensive reasons for denied request: *the ignorance of our asking, our use of prayer in fields where it does not belong,* and *the unreadiness of our own lives to receive the good we seek.* There are many people who have a thoughtless and unauthorized belief in the power of prayer to get things for themselves. They forget the searching condition put on all petition, that it must be in Christ's name (John 14:13; 16:23, 24,

26). No hurried addition of "For Jesus' sake" appended to a prayer can satisfy this deep and spiritual demand. Petition must be in accordance with the divine will and in harmony with Christ's spirit; it must be wise in itself and must come from a life persistent in its desires and unselfish in its purposes, before that law of prayer can be satisfied. To pray in Christ's name is nothing less than the acceptance of St. Augustine's attitude when he cried: "O Lord, grant that I may do thy will as if it were my will; so that thou mayest do my will as if it were thy will." Prayer is not magic, and it is a fortunate thing for us that Trumbull's word is true, alike to Scripture and experience, that so far as petition is concerned "Prayer is not to be depended on, but God is!"

There is one sense, however, in which answer to prayer can always be depended on, if a man has kept his life at all in harmony with God. *Even when God cannot answer affirmatively the man's petition he can answer the man.* Paul's petition for relief from his physical distress was not affirmatively answered, but Paul was answered. He went out from that denied request, thrice repeated, with a reply from God that put fortitude and courage into him: "My grace is sufficient for thee: for my power is made perfect in weakness" (II Cor. 12:9). God always answers true prayer in one of two ways—"No good prayer ever comes weeping home." For either he changes the circumstances or he supplies sufficient power to overcome them; he answers either the petition or the man. As Luther put it, "A Christian knows that he is not refused what he has prayed for, and finds, in fact, that he is helped in all troubles . . . and that God gives him power to bear his troubles and to overcome them: which is just the same thing as taking his trouble away from him, and making it no longer misfortune or distress, seeing it has been overcome."

This truth explains such amazing statements as Adoniram Judson, for example, made at the close of his life: "I never prayed sincerely and earnestly for anything, but it came; at some time—no matter at how distant a day—somehow, in some shape—probably the last I should have devised—it came." But Judson had prayed for entrance into India and had been compelled to go to Burmah; he had prayed for his wife's life, and had buried both her and his two children; he had prayed for release from the King of Ava's prison and had lain there months, chained and miserable. Scores of Judson's petitions had gone without an affirmative answer. But *Judson* always had

been answered. He had been upheld, guided, reenforced; unforeseen
doors had opened through the very trials he sought to avoid; and the
deep desires of his life were being accomplished not in his way but
beyond his way. He meant by his assertion of the unfailing power of
prayer what Paul meant when he cried, "My God shall supply every
need" (Phil. 4:19). Yes, even the Master faced denied petition. "Let
the cup pass," was a cry that could not be granted. But Jesus himself
was greatly answered in the Garden. The request was denied, but as
our Lord goes out to face Pilate and the cross, with a loyalty to his
Cause that no temptation can relax, a steadiness that no suffering
can shake, a magnanimity that neither nails nor spear nor gibe can
embitter, who can measure what in prayer has been done for the
Man?

SUGGESTIONS FOR THOUGHT AND DISCUSSION

Why are prayers unanswered?

What would happen if all petitions were granted?

If the course of events were decided alone in accordance with the
petitions to God by men, what kind of a world would it be?

To what extent would any individual be willing to have his
prayers answered?

What is the effect upon personal character of a religion that sub-
stitutes begging for honest work?

Under what circumstances do you think God would grant a petition for definite help in securing something which a man might get
by his own intellect and work?

*To what extent is it possible for a man's "petition" to be denied and
his "prayer" still to be answered?*

If we ask God for something in how far is it an answer to this
petition to be given the opportunity and direction to answer the
petition for ourselves?

In response to his petition to be relieved from "the thorn in the
flesh," which do you think presented the greater value to Paul—the
granting of his actual petition or the answer which he received?

If all petitions were unanswered, would it still be worth while to
pray?

Why are answers to prayer deferred?

What prerequisites does a wise father require of his sons before granting them their share of the inheritance? What light does this throw upon the answer to a petition being deferred by God?

Why did Jesus suggest the necessity of importunity in prayer?

What does the New Testament mean when it speaks of praying "in Christ's name"?

What is the difference between "answering a petition" and "answering a man"? Have any of my prayers really been unanswered?

CHAPTER VIII

Prayer as Dominant Desire

DAILY READINGS

First Day, Eighth Week

And God hath set some in the church, first apostles, secondly prophets, thirdly teachers, then miracles, then gifts of healings, helps, governments, divers kinds of tongues. Are all apostles? are all prophets? are all teachers, are all workers of miracles? have all gifts of healings? do all speak with tongues? do all interpret? But desire earnestly the greater gifts. And moreover a most excellent way show I unto you. If I speak with the tongues of men and of angels, but have not love, I am become sounding brass, or a clanging cymbal.—I Cor. 12:28-13:1.

Note the unfortunate break in this great passage made by a new chapter's beginning. The thirteenth chapter on love should always be read as an explanation of the verse in the twelfth chapter, "Desire earnestly the greater gifts."

Many reasons for unreality in prayer we have noted, such as perversity of mood, or failure to grasp the individual love of God, or wilful alienation of the life in sin. With one of the deepest troubles in our praying, however, we have not dealt. *Our prayers are often unreal because they do not represent what in our inward hearts we sincerely crave.* We ask God for the "greater gifts" which we do not "desire earnestly." For example we pray against some *evil habit* in our lives, while at the same time we refuse to give up the practices that make the habit easy, or the companionships in which the habit thrives. We go through the form of entreating God to save us from the sin, but we do not want the answer enough to burn the bridges across which the sin continually comes. Our petition is a lame and ineffective whim without driving power. Said "Chinese" Gordon: "I have been thinking over our feelings and how often it is that we are so very insincere even in prayer. . . . We pray for power to give up a certain habit, say evil speaking, and, at the moment of so praying, we have a thought of evil against some one, and we, as it were, whisper to that thought, 'By and by I will attend to you, not now,' and we go on praying against the very act we intend in our hearts to do. All this is insincere and dishonoring."

O God, whose Spirit searcheth all things, and whose love beareth all things, encourage us to draw near to Thee in sincerity and in truth. Save us from a worship of the lips while our hearts are far away. Save us from the useless labour of attempting to conceal ourselves from Thee who searchest the heart.

Enable us to lay aside all those cloaks and disguises which we wear in the light of day and here to bare ourselves, with all our weakness, disease and sin, naked to Thy sight.

Make us strong enough to bear the vision of the truth, and to have done with all falsehood, pretence, and hypocrisy, so that we may see things as they are, and fear no more.

Enable us to look upon the love which has borne with us and the heart that suffers for us. Help us to acknowledge our dependence on the purity that abides our uncleanness, the patience that forgives our faithlessness, the truth that forbears all our falsity and compromise. And may we have the grace of gratitude, and the desire to dedicate ourselves to Thee. Amen.—W. E. Orchard.

Second Day, Eighth Week

Therefore is the kingdom of heaven likened unto a certain king, who would make a reckoning with his servants. And when he had begun to reckon, one was brought unto him, that owed him ten thousand talents. . . . And the lord of that servant, being moved with compassion, released him, and forgave him the debt. But that servant went out, and found one of his fellow-servants, who owed him a hundred shillings: and he laid hold on him, and took him by the throat, saying, Pay what thou owest. So his fellow-servant fell down and besought him, saying, Have patience with me, and I will pay thee. And he would not: but went and cast him into prison,

till he should pay that which was due. So when his fellow-servants saw what was done, they were exceeding sorry, and came and told unto their lord all that was done. Then his lord called him unto him, and saith to him, Thou wicked servant, I forgave thee all that debt, because thou besoughtest me: shouldest not thou also have had mercy on thy fellow-servant, even as I had mercy on thee? And his lord was wroth, and delivered him to the tormentors, till he should pay all that was due. So shall also my heavenly Father do unto you, if ye forgive not every one his brother from your hearts. —Matt. 18:23, 24, 27-35.

The unreality of our praying may be illustrated in our petitions for *forgiveness*. Nothing may be more superficial than a request for pardon; nothing can be more searching than a genuine experience of penitence. A boy who has sinned and faces the consequence may have a momentary spell of regret; he naturally wishes to have the slate wiped clean. But to be sincerely sorry for his evil itself, rather than for its consequences; to be ashamed of his failure, so that he feels himself a brother of all sinners, and like Richard Baxter, could say of a murderer going to execution, "There but for the grace of God goes Richard Baxter!"—how penetrating an experience is that! Consider this expression of penitence from Tagore, the Bengali poet:

"I came out alone on my way to my tryst. But who is this that follows me in the silent dark?
I move aside to avoid his presence, but I escape him not.
He makes the dust rise from the earth with his swagger; he adds his loud voice to every word that I utter.
He is my own little self, my lord, he knows no shame; but I am ashamed to come to thy door in his company."

A man so sincerely ashamed of himself will seek forgiveness and renewal, with a genuine desire that will make his supplications real, and by the very vividness of his own sense of guilt will find it impossible to be unforgiving to any other man. Read again today's Scripture, and consider the Master's insistence on that kind of genuineness in our prayers for pardon.

O Searcher of hearts, Thou knowest us better than we know ourselves, and seest the sins which our sinfulness hides from us. Yet even our own conscience beareth witness against us, that we often slumber

*on our appointed watch; that we walk not always lovingly with each
other, and humbly with Thee; and we withhold that entire sacrifice
of ourselves to Thy perfect will, without which we are not crucified
with Christ, or sharers in His redemption. Oh, look upon our contri-
tion, and lift up our weakness, and let the dayspring yet arise within
our hearts, and bring us healing, strength, and joy. Day by day may
we grow in faith, in self-denial, in charity, in heavenly-mindedness.
And then, mingle us at last with the mighty host of Thy redeemed
for evermore. Amen.*—James Martineau (1805-1900).

Third Day, Eighth Week

Holy Father, keep them in thy name which thou hast given me,
that they may be one, even as we are. While I was with them, I
kept them in thy name which thou hast given me: and I guarded
them, and not one of them perished, but the son of perdition; that
the scripture might be fulfilled. But now I come to thee; and these
things I speak in the world, that they may have my joy made full
in themselves. I have given them thy word; and the world hated
them, because they are not of the world, even as I am not of the
world. I pray not that thou shouldest take them from the world,
but that thou shouldest keep them from the evil one. They are not
of the world, even as I am not of the world. Sanctify them in the
truth: thy word is truth. As thou didst send me into the world, even
so sent I them into the world. And for their sakes I sanctify myself,
that they themselves also may be sanctified in truth. Neither for
these only do I pray, but for them also that believe on me through
their word; that they may all be one; even as thou, Father, art in
me, and I in thee, that they also may be in us: that the world may
believe that thou didst send me.—John 17:11-21.

Consider another way in which we pray insincerely. We go
through the form of praying for our *friends*. It seems the right thing
to do, and it gives us at least a momentary glow of unselfishness.
But the prayer does not so rise from a controlling desire for our
friends' good, that we can be counted on all that day to be thoughtful about their needs, sensitive to their feelings, generous to their
faults, glad of their success, and helpful to our utmost in their
service. We often do not really *care* enough about our friends, so
that our supplication for them has vital meaning for us and, therefore, for God. As Nolan Rice Best has expressed it, "Like the su-

preme court of our land, the Supreme Court of heaven passes on no
hypothetical matters; the petitioner must have a real case in order
to obtain attention."

Think of the Master's love for his disciples, of the ways he revealed
it, of the lengths to which he willingly went in being true to it. The
reality of this intercessory prayer in John's seventeenth chapter goes
back to the genuineness of the love out of which it came. The prayer
actually represented what the Master sacrificially desired.

*O blessed Lord and Saviour, who hast commanded us to love one
another, grant us grace that, having received Thine undeserved
bounty, we may love every man in Thee and for Thee. We implore
Thy clemency for all; but especially for the friends whom Thy love
has given to us. Love Thou them, O Thou fountain of love, and
make them to love Thee with all their heart, with all their mind,
and with all their soul, that those things only which are pleasing to
Thee they may will, and speak, and do. And though our prayer is
cold, because our charity is so little fervent, yet Thou art rich in
mercy. Measure not to them Thy goodness by the dulness of our
devotion; but as Thy kindness surpasseth all human affection, so let
Thy hearing transcend our prayer. Do Thou to them what is expe-
dient for them, according to Thy will, that they, being always and
everywhere ruled and protected by Thee, may attain in the end to
everlasting life; and to Thee, with the Father and the Holy Spirit,
be all honour and praise for ever and ever. Amen.*—Anselm (1033-
1109).

Fourth Day, Eighth Week

If I have withheld the poor from their desire,
Or have caused the eyes of the widow to fail,
Or have eaten my morsel alone,
And the fatherless hath not eaten thereof. . . .
If I have seen any perish for want of clothing,
Or that the needy had no covering;
If his loins have not blessed me,
And if he hath not been warmed with the fleece of my sheep;
If I have lifted up my hand against the fatherless,
Because I saw my help in the gate:
Then let my shoulder fall from the shoulder-blade,
And mine arm be broken from the bone.—Job 31:16-22.

When a man can take words like these on his lips, as a description of his own life, he is prepared sincerely to pray for the *poor*. We often emphasize the fact that prayer is a powerful builder of character; but the other side of the truth is important, that *great character is essential to great praying*. A man with a small, mean, self-indulgent life cannot genuinely offer a noble prayer. This is the meaning of the saying that it is easy to commit the Lord's Prayer to memory, but difficult to learn it by heart. In any man's entreaty, no matter how great the words, only that much is real which is the expression of his character, the inward quality and habitual desire of his life. When, therefore, pity leads us to ask God's mercy on the poor, the value of our praying depends on the controlling power of that good desire in our lives. Does the supplication come out of an inward devotion that is to us of serious concern? Can God see in our habitual, systematic care for the poor and support of the agencies that help them, the proof of our prayer's sincerity?

We beseech Thee, Lord and Master, to be our help and succour. Save those who are in tribulation; have mercy on the lonely; lift up the fallen; show Thyself unto the needy; heal the ungodly; convert the wanderers of Thy people; feed the hungry; raise up the weak; comfort the faint-hearted. Let all the peoples know that Thou art God alone, and Jesus Christ is Thy Son, and we are Thy people and the sheep of Thy pasture; for the sake of Christ Jesus. Amen.— St. Clement of Rome (90 A. D.).

Fifth Day, Eighth Week

Now there were at Antioch, in the church that was there, prophets and teachers, Barnabas, and Symeon that was called Niger, and Lucius of Cyrene, and Manaen the foster-brother of Herod the tetrarch, and Saul. And as they ministered to the Lord, and fasted, the Holy Spirit said, Separate me Barnabas and Saul for the work whereunto I have called them. Then, when they had fasted and prayed and laid their hands on them, they sent them away. So they, being sent forth by the Holy Spirit, went down to Seleucia; and from thence they sailed to Cyprus.—Acts 13:1-4.

Note how this first missionary tour of Paul and his companions was conceived in the spirit of prayer and furthered by prayer's power. We too have prayed for *missions*. Perhaps we have personal friends on the foreign field and that fact has quickened our sense of obligations to pray for the Cause. But the plain fact often is that while we are offering prayers, we are offering nothing else. We make supplication a substitute for devotion. We do not give to missions with any deep sense of stewardship, but rather treat the Cause of the Kingdom as a charity, to which an occasional dole from our surplus is sufficient. In our inmost desires we are not devotedly set on the triumph of Christ's cause, so that we seek information about missions, make as generous gifts as we can, and put personal service into strengthening the church as the "home base." In our petitions for the missionaries, how often, as Friar Lawrence phrases it, we are "fooling ourselves with trivial devotions."

O great Lord of the harvest, send forth, we beseech Thee, labourers into the harvest of the world, that the grain which is even now ripe may not fall and perish through our neglect. Pour forth Thy sanctifying Spirit on our fellow Christians abroad, and Thy converting grace on those who are living in darkness. Raise up, we beseech Thee, a devout ministry among the native believers, that all Thy people being knit together in one body, in love, Thy Church may grow up into the measure of the stature of the fulness of Christ; through Him who died, and rose again for us all, the same Jesus Christ our Lord. Amen.—Bishop Milman (1791-1868).

Sixth Day, Eighth Week

Pray for the peace of Jerusalem:
They shall prosper that love thee.
Peace be within thy walls,
And prosperity within thy palaces.
For my brethren and companions' sakes,
I will now say, Peace be within thee.
For the sake of the house of Jehovah our God
I will seek thy good.—Psalm 122:6-9.

In the time of a great war, nothing is more natural than prayer for *peace*. But of all petitions that arise for peace, how many represent deep and transforming devotion of the life to the cause of human brotherhood? Men pray for peace, and still retain and express those racial prejudices that are one of the most prolific causes of war. They ask for human brotherhood to come, but they are most unbrotherly to the foreigner within their own communities. Women piously frame petitions in behalf of the day when there shall be no "barbarian, Scythian, bondman, freeman; but Christ is all, and in all," but all the while they violate every Christian principle in their dealings with their servants, their social inferiors, or the aliens of their city. Their prayers are long-range dreams that do not touch their lives. And least of all do many of us, when we pray for peace, purge our own hearts of that rancor that lies behind all war. "Let all bitterness, and wrath, and anger, and clamor, and railing, be put away from you, with all malice: and be ye kind one to another, tender-hearted, forgiving each other, even as God also in Christ forgave you" (Eph. 4:31).

O Lord, since first the blood of Abel cried to Thee from the ground that drank it, this earth of Thine has been defiled with the blood of man shed by his brother's hand, and the centuries sob with the ceaseless horror of war. Ever the pride of kings and the covetousness of the strong have driven peaceful nations to slaughter. Ever the songs of the past and the pomp of armies have been used to inflame the passions of the people. Our spirit cries out to Thee in revolt against it, and we know that our righteous anger is answered by Thy holy wrath.

Break Thou the spell of the enchantments that make the nations drunk with the lust of battle and draw them on as willing tools of death. Grant us a quiet and steadfast mind when our own nation clamors for vengeance or aggression. Strengthen our sense of justice and our regard for the equal worth of other peoples and races. Grant to the rulers of nations faith in the possibility of peace through justice, and grant to the common people a new and stern enthusiasm for the cause of peace. Bless our soldiers and sailors for their swift obedience and their willingness to answer to the call of duty, but inspire them none the less with a hatred of war, and may they never for love of private glory or advancement provoke its coming. May our young men still rejoice to die for their country with the valor of their fathers, but teach our age nobler methods of matching our strength and more effective ways of giving our life for the flag.

O Thou strong Father of all nations, draw all Thy great family together with an increasing sense of our common blood and destiny,

*that peace may come on earth at last, and Thy sun may shed its
light rejoicing on a holy brotherhood of peoples.*—Walter Rauschenbusch.

Seventh Day, Eighth Week

And it came to pass after these things, that Naboth the Jezreelite
had a vineyard, which was in Jezreel, hard by the palace of Ahab
king of Samaria. And Ahab spake unto Naboth, saying, Give me
thy vineyard, that I may have it for a garden of herbs, because it is
near unto my house; and I will give thee for it a better vineyard
than it: or, if it seem good to thee, I will give thee the worth of it
in money. And Naboth said to Ahab, Jehovah forbid it me, that I
should give the inheritance of my fathers unto thee. And Ahab
came into his house heavy and displeased because of the word which
Naboth the Jezreelite had spoken to him; for he had said, I will not
give thee the inheritance of my fathers. And he laid him down upon
his bed, and turned away his face, and would eat no bread.—
I Kings 21:1-4.

Supposing that Ahab had said his prayers that night, would it
have made much difference what he said in praying? Imagine him
rehearsing some formal petitions learned in his childhood; *would
that have been his real prayer?* It is clear that Ahab's demand on
life that night was simply his covetous desire for Naboth's vineyard.
No formal, proper, pious supplication addressed to God could have
hidden from the divine insight this deeper fact, that what Ahab
really wanted was his neighbor's field. Consider how often God must
so look through our conventionally proper petitions, and in our
hearts perceive our unvoiced but controlling wants—sometimes as
mean, selfish, covetous as Ahab's. These are the deep *prayers* of our
lives—our hearts are set upon them—and God is not deceived when
we tell him in pious phrases that we wish his blessing. Let us consider
this week what our hearts really are set on, what are our chief ambitions and desires.

*O Eternal God, sanctify my body and soul, my thoughts and my
intentions, my words and actions, that whatsoever I shall think, or
speak, or do, may be by me designed for the glorification of Thy
Name, and by Thy blessing, it may be effective and successful in the
work of God, according as it can be capable. Lord, turn my necessi-*

ties into virtue; the works of nature into the works of grace; by making them orderly, regular, temperate; and let no pride or self-seeking, no covetousness or revenge, no little ends and low imaginations, pollute my spirit, and unhallow any of my words and actions; but let my body be a servant of my spirit, and both body and spirit servants of Jesus; that, doing all things for Thy glory here, I may be partaker of Thy glory hereafter, through Jesus Christ our Lord. Amen.—Jeremy Taylor (1613-1667).

COMMENT FOR THE WEEK

I

Hitherto we have spoken of prayer as a definitely religious act. In using the word we thought of hearts bowed in the presence of God; we thought of shut doors, bent knees, reverent spirits. *But in this chapter we must sink down into that realm of human desire, which, like an ocean under separate waves, lies beneath all specially religious petitions.*

At least during the early portion of this chapter we must think of prayer as quite separable from religion; we must ask not only what our desires are when we bow before God, but what our dominant aims are in daily business; what we are really after in our innermost ambitions; what is our demand on life. Prayer, in this more inclusive sense, is the settled craving of a man's heart, *good or bad,* his inward love and determining desire. When the prodigal in Jesus' parable said, "Father, give me the portion of thy substance that falleth to me," he was in a real sense praying. His innermost ambition was there expressed. His heart was set on gaining the means that in the end would be his ruin. It was a prayer resolutely directed toward evil, but it was prayer. In this sense, Columbus' search for America was prayer; Edison's long attempt to find the secret of incandescence was prayer; Paul's ambition to found Christian churches and Napoleon's ambition to rule Europe both were prayers. Not alone the woman who pleads with the reluctant judge for justice, but the prodigal seeking from his father the means of dissipation, is praying; and any man who after money or fame or pleasure insistently directs his course, has in his dominant desire the prayer that shapes his life. We must accept for a while the fruitful definition which Mrs. Browning gives us, "Every *wish,* with God, is a prayer."

II

One immediate result of this point of view is a clear perception that *everybody is praying.* Prayer regarded as a definite act of approach to God may be shut out from any life. But prayer regarded as desire, exercised in any realm and for anything, at once includes us all. In this general sense we pray without ceasing. We are hunger-points in the universe; the elemental fact in every human life is desire. To a man who disclaims any act of prayer we may retort, "Your life *is* an organized prayer: Your body craves food, your mind craves knowledge, your affection craves friendship, your spirit craves peace and hope. You do not pray? Rather every stroke of work and every purposeful thought are endeavors to satisfy inward prayers."

Ordinarily prayer is regarded as the act of a man's best hours. *But in this deeper sense men pray in their worst hours too.* Prayer may be either heavenly or devilish. When we think of a man's dominant desire as in very truth his prayer, we see that Gehazi, with covetous eyes following Naaman to filch his wealth, is praying; that David, with licentious heart putting Uriah at the front of the battle, is praying; that the prodigal seeking the means of his own ruin is praying. None ever found heaven, here or anywhere, without prayer —the uplift of a settled desire after God and righteousness. And none ever found hell, here or anywhere, without prayer—the dead set and insistent craving of the heart after evil. In any group of men, you may not in this sense divide those who pray from those who do not. All are praying the prayer of dominant desire. The great question is: what are they after? what is their demand on life?

III

It is to be noted, also, that prayer in this sense is the inward measure of any man's quality. Living beings reveal their grade in the scale of existence by their wants. Inanimate things want nothing. Stones and clods are undisturbed by any sense of lack. The faintest glimmering of life, however, brings in the reign of want. Even in some one-celled amoeba rolling about in search of food, the presence of life means a hunger which is the rudiment of prayer. And from these dim beginnings of instinctive need to the spiritual demands of sage and saint, the extent and quality of a being's wants are a good measure of his life.

In the difference between a savage, wanting nothing but nakedness, a straw-hut, and raw food to content him, and one of us, demanding conveniences that lay tribute on the ends of the earth, our material progress can be measured. In the difference between an African dwarf, with no interests beyond his jungle's edge, and a modern scientist beating the wings of his enquiry against the uttermost bars of the universe, we can gauge our intellectual growth. In the difference between a pagan with his fetish, and Paul saying of his life with Christ, "I press on," our spiritual enlargement is measured. The greater a man is, the wider and deeper and finer are his desires. His prayer is the measure of him. What it takes to meet his need is the gauge of his size. Men come into life as they move into strange cities and at once begin praying. Some ask for the city's places of vulgar amusement or of vice; some for the best music and the finest art; some for low companionship, others for good friends; and some for the centers of social service and the temples of God. So each man prays and as he prays he reveals his quality. *No man can escape the prayer of dominant desire, nor evade the inevitable measurement of his life by his prayer.*

IV

This truth becomes very serious when we face a further development of it: *that the prayer of dominant desire always tends to attain its object.* This is true, in the first place, because a central craving organizes all the faculties of our lives about itself and sets mind and hands to do its bidding. Of the three ways in which men cooperate with God, working, thinking, and praying, a cursory view might suggest that praying is a somewhat superfluous addition; that, at least, the other two plainly belong first in importance. *On the contrary the prayer of dominant desire habitually precedes thought and work.* We think and labor because in our innermost heart we have prayed first, because some Desire is in us, calling to our minds, "Come, bring me this!" and ordering our hands, "Go bring me that!" Desire is the elemental force in human experience.

A man wants money. That is his real demand on life—his prayer. How his mind, then, puts on servile livery to wait on his dominant desire! How quick his wit becomes, how sinewy his thought in the service of his prayer! Wherever men concentrate their wills, apply their minds and submit to toil, back of this visible consequence is dominant desire. If Bismarck stops at nothing in amalgamating the German Empire, an ambition is in the saddle—"You may hang me," he said, "so long as the rope you do it with binds Germany to the Prussian throne." And if Burns writes incomparable Scotch lyrics, we must trace his labor back to his prayer:

> "E'en then a *wish* (I mind its pow'r),
>   A wish that to my latest hour
>   Shall strongly heave my breast,
>   That I for poor auld Scotland's sake
>   Some usefu' plan or book could make,
>   Or sing a song at least."

Dominant desire gathers up the scattered faculties, concenters the mind, nerves the will, and drives hard toward the issue. It always tends to achieve its end. As John Burroughs put it, "If you have a thing in mind, it is not long before you have it in hand."

This prayer of dominant desire, however, tends to achieve its object, not merely because it concentrates the powers within the man, but because *it calls into alliance with it forces from without the man.* Wherever there is low pressure in the atmosphere, thither the wind rushes to fill the need. So the cravings of men create low-pressure areas and, from without, help blows in to the fulfilment of their desires. This is easily illustrated in the social life, for in every enterprise now on foot in the world, men are endeavoring to supply other men's desires—churches to meet the desire for worship, saloons to meet the craving for drink, schools to supply the thirst for knowledge. Behind every organization lies a craving. Human wants are the open bays that call the sea of human effort in.

This truth is just as evident in the life of the individual. When a man craves vicious pleasure, low companions inevitably drift to him from every side; low books that pure minds pass unobserved, flow in to satisfy his appetite. His prayer creates a call that is answered by everything kindred to his want. As a whirlwind catches up the adjacent air into its vortex, so a man's desire calls in the congenial forces of his environment. To the prodigal, doubtless, every evil influence in the village came by spiritual gravitation to further his evil purpose, until at last his dominant desire *drew his father in.* The very patrimony which was meant to be his blessing he used in furtherance of his controlling passion until it proved his curse. To translate the story at once into the terms of our experience with God, the universe itself responds to a man's insistent demands upon it. Even the forces of the spiritual world align themselves, however reluctantly, with a man's controlling prayer. He can create a back eddy in the river of God's will, and the very waters that would have helped him go straight on, will now swirl around his dominant desire.

Here, then, is one of the most revealing and startling aspects in which the meaning of prayer may be considered: *we all are praying the prayer of dominant desire, our quality is measured by it; and because it both engages in its service our inward powers and calls to its furtherance forces from without, it tends with certainty to achieve its end.*

v

When from this general consideration of prayer as desire, we move up to the more usual thought of prayer as the soul's definite approach to God, we gain outlooks on our subject that no other road so well affords. We see clearly that *many of the speeches addressed to God that we have called our prayers are not real prayers at all.* They are not our dominant desires. They do not express the inward set and determination of our lives. What we pray for in the closet is not the thing that daily we are seeking with undiscourageable craving. It is not difficult to pray with the *lips* for renewed character and serviceable life, for social justice and the triumph of the Gospel. The Bible shows us in many a familiar passage what we *ought* to pray for. The liturgies of the churches too are beautifully eloquent with prayers that welled up from sincerely aspiring hearts, and we readily can frame petitions that copy the letter of the churches' prayers. A man in this superficial sense may gain the trick of public supplication. His prayers are eloquent and beautiful, they are verbal aspiration after most worthy things. But as with "Solomon's Prayer" at the dedication of the temple, there is an appalling hiatus between the requests publicly made and the manifest desires of the man who prays. *Prayer that is not dominant desire is too weak to achieve any-thing.* Any loitering student can cheaply pray to be learned; any idler in the market place can pray to be rich; any irresolute dodger of duty can pray for a vigorous character. But such praying is not really prayer.

> "Prayer is the *soul's sincere desire,*
> Uttered or unexpressed,
> The motion of a hidden *fire*
> That trembles in the breast."

This perception of the nature of true prayer as dominant desire addressed to God, lights up two important matters. For one thing it adds a significant contribution to our thought on unanswered prayer. *It suggests that while a man's outward petition may be denied, his dominant desire, which is his real prayer, may be granted.* Parents for example pray for their children's character and usefulness. They ask that godliness and public-mindedness may make their sons and daughters men and women of spiritual distinction. Such supplications are eminently worthy; but too often, proper as they are, they do not represent the parents' dominant desire. The real wish that controls decisions, that creates the atmosphere of the home and shapes the character of the children, is the parents' ambition for the children's wealth or social success. There lies the family's masterful craving. Now as between the spoken prayer and the dominant desire, is there any question which will be answered? The fact is that the *real* prayer of that family tends inevitably to be answered. Many a man would have to confess that for all his denied petition, he had gotten what his heart was inwardly set upon. The controlling passion in any life draws an answer, sometimes with appalling certainty.

Men are given to complaining of unanswered prayer, but *the great disasters are due to answered prayers.* The trouble with men is that so often they *do* get what they want. When the prodigal in the far country came to himself, friends gone, reputation gone, will-power almost gone, to find himself poor, hungry, feeding swine, he was suffering from the consequence of an answered prayer, a dominant desire fulfilled. So Lot wanted Sodom, and got it; Ahab craved Naboth's vineyard, and seized it; Judas desired the thirty pieces, and obtained them. The Bible is full of answered prayers that ruined men. The power of dominant desire is terrific. Again and again in history we see the old truth come true: "He gave them their request, but sent leanness into their soul!" (Psalm 106:15).

> "O Gracious Lord, how blind we are,
> On our own ruin bent!
> Make not thine answer to our prayer
> Our bitterest punishment!

"For to importunate approach
Persistent in its wrong,
Thou grantest its deluded wish
To make thy warning strong."

VI

*This perception of the nature of prayer as dominant desire also
lights up one of the most notable causes of failure in praying—insincerity.* The Master laid reiterated emphasis upon sincerity in prayer.
He meant that the petition offered must be the genuine overflow of
inward desire. The fault of the Pharisees who prayed on the corners
was not that they were asking for unworthy things. Their petitions
were doubtless excellent, springing out of scriptural ideas and
couched in scriptural language. But the prayers did not represent
the inward and determining wishes of the men. The petitions were
not sincere. The lives of the Pharisees blatantly advertised that their
habitual ambitions did not tally with their occasional supplications.
When the Master bids us make prayer private, to think of God
when we pray as "the Father who seeth in secret," to use no futile
and repetitious formulas but to go at once to the pith of our want
(Matt. 6:5ff), he is making a plea for sincerity. Prayer to him is the
heart, with all its most genuine and worthy desires aflame, rising up
to lay hold on God. It is no affair of hasty words at the fag-end of
a day, no form observed in deference to custom, no sop to conscience to ease us from the sense of religious obligations unfulfilled.
Prayer is the central and determining force of a man's life. *Prayer is
dominant desire, calling God into alliance.*

The fact that we do not stand on street corners to perform our
devotions ought not to blind us to the subtle temptation by which,
even in private, we are led into theatrical, insincere praying. We
pray as we think we *ought* to. We ask for blessings that we feel are
properly to be asked for, graces that we *should* want, whether we do
or not. We mask ourselves behind an imaginary personage—ourselves disguised in court clothes and asking from God the things
which we presume God would like to be asked to give. We cry as St.
Augustine did, "O Lord, make me pure"; and then we hear our real
self add as his did, "but *not now!*" How much such praying there is
and how utterly ineffective! It is not real. We have not at the center
of our lives controlling desires so worthy that we can ask God to

further them and so earnest that our prayers are the spontaneous
utterance of their urgency.

In the last chapter we spoke of such petitions as "Thy kingdom
come," which for nearly twenty centuries has been the prayer of the
church. But how many have *really* prayed it? In how many has it
been the dominant desire? Economists describe what they call "effective demand." It is the demand of those who not only need com-
modities, but who are willing and able to pay the price. Only when
a petition becomes an "effective demand" is it real prayer. When a
man rehearses all the blessings he has prayed for himself and the
world, he may well go on to ask whether he really wishes the prayers
granted. Is he willing to pay the price? The great servants of the
Kingdom in history always have been men of prayer and the impli-
cation is sometimes suggested that praying would make us similarly
serviceable. But this essential element should never be forgotten, that
the great servants of the Kingdom were men of powerful prayer
because they were men of dominant desires for whose fulfilment
they were willing to sacrifice anything. Paul, Carey, Livingstone, and
all their spiritual kin praying for the triumph of Christ with all
their hearts and hurling their lives after their prayers; St. Augustine
at last *really* praying for purity, until the answer involved tearing
loose the dearest ties of his past life—these are examples of costly
praying which achieves results. This is not prayer called in to eke
out what is lacking in an otherwise contented life; this is life cen-
tering in and swung round prayer like planets round the sun. Prayer
becomes serious business when it becomes dominant desire. We stand
there at life's center, at the springs of its motive and the sources of
its power.

A cursory reading of the Beatitudes awakens surprise because
prayer is not mentioned there. How could the Master sum up the
benedictions of the spiritual life and omit prayer from his thought?
Turn to them again, then, and read more deeply. The Master put
prayer into the Beatitudes in one of the greatest descriptions to be
found in the Bible: "Blessed are they that *hunger and thirst* after
righteousness: for they shall be filled" (Matt. 5:6). Prayer is hunger
and thirst. *Prayer is our demand on life, elevated, purified, and
aware of a Divine Alliance.*

SUGGESTIONS FOR THOUGHT AND DISCUSSION

What is the relation between prayer and a person's dominant desires and purposes?

How far does prayer represent the real purpose and desire of the man?

When do the words spoken in prayer fail to represent the real prayers?

How far can a man's character be measured by his prayers?

What is the difference between outward petition and a dominant desire of a life?

What effect upon the answer to prayer has a person's dominant desire?

Can prayer which does not represent dominant desire be answered? Why or why not?

What made the difference in the prayer for forgiveness of the servant who owed ten thousand talents and the one who owed one hundred shillings? When has a person a right to expect an answer to a prayer for forgiveness?

How far was the first missionary tour of Paul the result of prayer? What is the difference between offering a prayer for missions and offering ourselves?

When is a nation's prayer for peace sincere? To what extent does prejudice against other classes and nations interfere with an effective prayer for peace?

When are we justified in praying for the poor? for our friends? for forgiveness? for world brotherhood? for missions?

Are all prayers representing dominant desire answered?

When is prayer sincere?

Why did the Master denounce the prayers of the Pharisees?

Why does lack of time for meditation make for insincerity in prayer?

When does a person really pray "Thy kingdom come"?

What is the relation of procrastination to the inefficacy of prayer?

What light do the Beatitudes throw upon the prerequisite of answered prayer?

What makes the difference between a petition addressed to God and a sincere prayer?

What makes for insincerity in prayer?

What is the relation of dominant desire to sincerity in prayer?

How can I make my prayers sincerely represent my dominant desires?

CHAPTER IX

Prayer as a Battlefield

DAILY READINGS

First Day, Ninth Week

Behold, thou desirest truth in the inward parts;
And in the hidden part thou wilt make me to know wisdom.
Purify me with hyssop, and I shall be clean:
Wash me, and I shall be whiter than snow.
Make me to hear joy and gladness,
That the bones which thou hast broken may rejoice.
Hide thy face from my sins,
And blot out all mine iniquities.
Create in me a clean heart, O God;
And renew a right spirit within me.
Cast me not away from thy presence;
And take not thy holy Spirit from me.
Restore unto me the joy of thy salvation;
And uphold me with a willing spirit.
Then will I teach transgressors thy ways;
And sinners shall be converted unto thee.—Psalm 51:6-13.

The Psalmist is praying here for a cleansed and empowered personality. The secret place where he first offered these entreaties must have been to him a battlefield. There took place those inner struggles on whose issue moral purity and power depend. *Prayer is the innermost form of the fight for character.* As Clement of Alexandria in the second century, put it, "The aim of prayer is to attain the habit of goodness, so as no longer merely to have the things that are good, but rather to be good," and in our generation George Meredith restates the same truth, "Who rises from his prayer a better man, his prayer is answered." *The profoundest need of the world is clean, strong, devoted personality.* We are poor there—not in material prosperity or organizing skill or intellectual ingenuity, but in radiant, infectious, convincing personality. The real poverty is poverty of character, and that is due in how large a measure to the lack of those spiritual disciplines and fellowships which are included in genuine prayer! Let us consider this week the service of prayer as an inner battlefield on which the issues of character are settled.

O God, make perfect my love toward Thee and to my Redeemer and Justifier; give me a true and unfeigned love to all virtue and godliness, and to all Thy chosen people wheresoever they be dispersed throughout all the world; increase in me strength and victory against all temptations and assaults of the flesh, the world, and the devil, that according to Thy promise I be never further proved or tempted than Thou wilt give me strength to overcome. Give me grace to keep a good conscience; give me a pure heart and mind, and renew a right spirit within me. Amen.—Christian Prayers (1556).

Second Day, Ninth Week

And at even, when the sun did set, they brought unto him all that were sick, and them that were possessed with demons. And all the city was gathered together at the door. And he healed many that were sick with divers diseases, and cast out many demons; and he suffered not the demons to speak, because they knew him. And in the morning, a great while before day, he rose up and went out, and departed into a desert place, and there prayed. And Simon and they that were with him followed after him; and they found him, and say unto him, All are seeking thee. And he saith unto them, Let us go elsewhere into the next towns, that I may preach there also; for to this end came I forth. And he went into their synagogues throughout all Galilee, preaching and casting out demons. —Mark 1:32-39.

Was not this solitary prayer of the Master a battle for courage and strength to go on? It came between the crushing labors of Capernaum and the preaching tour that lay ahead; it came at a time when the storm of the Pharisees' wrath was gathering. If the Master needed the courage that comes in solitary prayer, can we well dispense with it? Many lives would be incalculably strengthened, their tone would be changed from anxious timidity to power, if they would learn the secret of this inner fellowship. It is said that Napoleon before a great battle would stand alone in his tent, and one by one the marshals and commanders of his armies would enter, grasp his hand in silence, and go out again—fired with a new courage and resolute in a new willingness to die for France. Some such effect those souls have felt who have learned the secret of prayer's power.

O Thou, who art the ever-blessed God, the underlying Peace of the world, and who wouldst draw all men into the companionship of Thy joy; speak, we beseech Thee, to this Thy servant, for whom we pray. Take him by the hand and say unto him, "Fear not; for I am with thee. I have called thee by my name; thou art mine." Put such a spirit of trust within him that all fear and foreboding shall be cast out, and that right reason and calm assurance may rule his thoughts and impulses. Let quietness and confidence be his strength. Reveal to him the vision of a universe guided and governed by Thy wise and loving care; and show him that around and about him are Thy unseen and beneficent powers. Lift up his whole being into communion with Thy life and thought. Let him ever remember that Thou dost not give to any the spirit of fearfulness, but a spirit of power and love and self-mastery. In this faith, grant, O Lord, that he may summon the energies of his soul against the miseries that cast him down. Give him courage, confidence, an untroubled heart, and a love that loves all creatures, great and small, for Thy love's sake. Amen.—Samuel McComb.

Third Day, Ninth Week

Finally, be strong in the Lord, and in the strength of his might. Put on the whole armor of God, that ye may be able to stand against the wiles of the devil. For our wrestling is not against flesh and blood, but against the principalities, against the powers, against the world-rulers of this darkness, against the spiritual hosts of wickedness in the heavenly places. Wherefore take up the whole armor of God, that ye may be able to withstand in the evil day, and, having done all, to stand. Stand therefore, having girded your loins

with truth, and having put on the breastplate of righteousness, and
having shod your feet with the preparation of the gospel of peace;
withal taking up the shield of faith, wherewith ye shall be able to
quench all the fiery darts of the evil one. And take the helmet of
salvation, and the sword of the Spirit, which is the sword of God:
with all prayer and supplication praying at all seasons in the Spirit,
and watching thereunto in all perseverance and supplication for all
the saints.—Eph. 6:10-18.

Note the surprising conclusion of this warlike passage. The man
is armed for conflict and then the climax reads "with all prayer . . .
praying." To the Apostle prayer evidently has a warlike aspect. He
is writing this passage in prison, where he needs *fortitude to endure.*
In prayer he finds the battlefield where he fights his fears and gains
enduring power that he may be able, "having done all, to stand."
How many people weakly give way in the face of trouble, lose their
spirit, fall into self-pity, and refuse to join that great succession of
God's people who have proved by the way they handled their
troubles, even more than by the way they handled their talents, what
God can do for a man of faith! It is said that in a newly invented
vacuum furnace everything in a log of wood that is destructible can
be consumed, leaving only an irreducible minimum that man's skill
is not yet great enough to burn. And we are told that that in-
destructible remainder is pure carbon, *every bit of which the tree
took from the sunlight through the leaves.* Many may think of
prayer as a strange way of gaining power to endure, but the in-
destructible elements of the soul, that cannot be crushed or consumed by adversity, do come from our spiritual fellowship with God.
Consider this prayer of Lady Jane Grey in her last imprisonment:

*O Merciful God, be Thou now unto me a strong tower of defence,
I humbly entreat Thee. Give me grace to await Thy leisure, and
patiently to bear what Thou doest unto me; nothing doubting or
mistrusting Thy goodness towards me; for Thou knowest what is
good for me better than I do. Therefore do with me in all things
what Thou wilt; only arm me, I beseech Thee, with Thine armour,
that I may stand fast; above all things, taking to me the shield of
faith; praying always that I may refer myself wholly to Thy will,
abiding Thy pleasure, and comforting myself in those troubles
which it shall please Thee to send me, seeing such troubles are*

profitable for me; and I am assuredly persuaded that all Thou doest cannot but be well; and unto Thee be all honour and glory. Amen.
—Lady Jane Grey (1537-1554).

Fourth Day, Ninth Week

Then was Jesus led up of the Spirit into the wilderness to be tempted of the devil. And when he had fasted forty days and forty nights, he afterward hungered. And the tempter came and said unto him, If thou art the Son of God, command that these stones become bread. But he answered and said, It is written, Man shall not live by bread alone, but by every word that proceedeth out of the mouth of God. Then the devil taketh him into the holy city; and he set him on the pinnacle of the temple, and saith unto him, If thou art the Son of God, cast thyself down: for it is written,

He shall give his angels charge concerning thee:
and,

On their hands they shall bear thee up,
Lest haply thou dash thy foot against a stone.

Jesus said unto him, Again it is written, Thou shalt not make trial of the Lord thy God. Again, the devil taketh him unto an exceeding high mountain, and showeth him all the kingdoms of the world, and the glory of them; and he said unto him, All these things will I give thee, if thou wilt fall down and worship me. Then saith Jesus unto him, Get thee hence, Satan: for it is written, Thou shalt worship the Lord thy God, and him only shalt thou serve. Then the devil leaveth him; and behold, angels came and ministered unto him.—Matt. 4:1-11.

These verses are the record of an inward struggle in which the Master fought out the purpose of his life. The use of Scripture, the continual reference in Jesus' words to God and God's claims on men, indicate the atmosphere of devotion in which this battle was fought. *Do we deal with our temptations in this high way?* Consider our besetting sins—temper, passion, irreverence or whatever other form of self-will we may most easily fall into, and think of the ways the habitual use of inward prayer would help us. How an improper story or a mean judgment withers on our lips if a fine, high-minded personality happens to join the circle! And what a cleansing effect takes place in our lives if we grow accustomed to usher God upon the scene when uncleanness or ill-temper or self-will appears! Gradually but surely those feelings and thoughts which are not comfortable when God is present disappear. The life grows clear of those tempers and attitudes that make spontaneous prayer impossible. "The devil leaveth him."

O Thou, who proclaimest liberty to the captives, and the opening of the prisons to them that are bound; we rejoice that Thou hast brought the soul of this Thy servant out of prison that he might praise Thy name. Thou didst inspire him with pure desires. Thou didst rouse him again and again from despair and didst sustain him in the fight for freedom. And now we bless Thee that Thou hast crowned his efforts with success. Abide with him and in him that henceforth he may bear the fruits of good living. So fill him with love and holiness, with courage and trust, that through all the coming days temptation will lose its power. Let the dead past bury its dead. Go with him into the new world of joy and peace and health. Inspire him with the resolve to do something for Thy sake, to tell another imprisoned soul what great things Thou hast done that, if it please Thee, he may have a double joy. Hear our thanksgiving and bless us through Jesus Christ, our Lord. Amen.—Samuel McComb.

Fifth Day, Ninth Week

Is any among you suffering? let him pray. Is any cheerful? let him sing praise. Is any among you sick? let him call for the elders of the church; and let them pray over him, anointing him with oil in the name of the Lord: and the prayer of faith shall save him that is sick, and the Lord shall raise him up; and if he have committed sins, it shall be forgiven him. Confess therefore your sins one to another, and pray one for another, that ye may be healed. The supplication of a righteous man availeth much in its working.— James 5:13-16.

Never more than in our day has the wisdom of this ancient advice been clear. *Prayer is the inner battlefield where men often conquer most effectually the false worries, trivial anxieties, morbid humors and all the unwholesome specters of the mind that irritate the spirit and make the body ill.* There they learn Paul's lesson, "In nothing be anxious; but in everything by prayer and supplication with thanksgiving let your requests be made known unto God. And the peace of God, which passeth all understanding, shall guard your hearts and your thoughts in Christ Jesus" (Phil. 4:6, 7). Dr. Hyslop, Superintendent of Bethlehem Royal Hospital, at the annual meeting of the British Medical Association in 1905, said: "As an alienist, and one whose whole life has been concerned with the sufferings of the mind, I would state that of all hygienic measures to counteract disturbed, sleep-depressed spirits, and all the miserable sequels of a distressed mind, I would undoubtedly give the first place to the simple habit of prayer."

Ever Blessed God, whose word is, "Peace, peace to him that is far off and to him that is near," fulfil Thy promise to this Thy servant for whom we pray. Rescue him from the misery of groundless fears and restless anxieties. Take him more and more out of himself, that duty may be no longer a drudgery but a delight. Lead him into the secret of Thy peace which quiets every misgiving and fills the heart with joy and confidence. Save him from the shame and emptiness of a hurried life. Grant him to possess his soul in patience. Amid the storms and stress of life, let him hear a deeper voice assuring him that Thou livest and that all is well. Strengthen him to do his daily work in quietness and confidence, fearing no tomorrow, nor the evil that it brings, for Thou art with him. And this we ask for Jesus Christ's sake. Amen.—Samuel McComb.

Sixth Day, Ninth Week

And he went forward a little, and fell on his face, and prayed, saying, My Father, if it be possible, let this cup pass away from me: nevertheless, not as I will, but as thou wilt.—Matt. 26:39.

Again a second time he went away, and prayed, saying, My Father, if this cannot pass away, except I drink it, thy will be done. —Matt. 26:42.

And he said, Abba, Father, all things are possible unto thee; remove this cup from me: howbeit not what I will, but what thou wilt.—Mark 14:36.

Father, if thou be willing, remove this cup from me: nevertheless not my will, but thine, be done.—Luke 22:42.

Consider the battlefield of Gethsemane. Was there ever a more eventful engagement than that? *It was a struggle for clear vision to see and strength to do the will of God.* Peter Annet, an old Deist, used to say that praying men are like sailors who have cast anchor on a rock, and who imagine they are pulling the rock to themselves, when they are really pulling themselves to the rock. But that is a caricature of what praying men at their best think. The Master here was deliberately trying to pull himself to the rock. That was the objective of the struggle in the garden. The will of God was settled; he wanted clearly to see it and strongly to be apprehended by it, and he called God in to fight the narrower self will that opposed the larger devotion. What a deep experience such praying brings into any life that knows it! As Phillips Brooks exclaimed: "God's mercy seat is no mere stall set by the vulgar road side, where every careless passer-by may put an easy hand out to snatch any glittering blessing that catches his eye. It stands in the holiest of holies. We can come to it only through veils and by altars of purification. To enter into it, we must enter into God."

O God, who hast in mercy taught us how good it is to follow the holy desires which Thou manifoldly puttest into our hearts, and how bitter is the grief of falling short of whatever beauty our minds behold, strengthen us, we beseech Thee, to walk steadfastly throughout life in the better path which our hearts once chose; and give us wisdom to tread it prudently in Thy fear, as well as cheerfully in Thy love; so that, having been faithful to Thee all the days of our life here, we may be able hopefully to resign ourselves into Thy hands hereafter. Amen.—Rowland Williams (1818-1870).

Seventh Day, Ninth Week

And I said, O my God, I am ashamed and blush to lift up my face to thee, my God; for our iniquities are increased over our head, and our guiltiness is grown up unto the heavens. Since the days of our fathers we have been exceeding guilty unto this day; and for our iniquities have we, our kings, and our priests, been delivered into the hand of the kings of the lands, to the sword, to captivity, and to plunder, and to confusion of face, as it is this day. . . . And now, O our God, what shall we say after this? for we have forsaken thy commandments . . . And after all that is come upon us for our evil deeds, and for our great guilt, seeing that thou our God hast punished us less than our iniquities deserve, and hast given us such

a remnant, shall we again break thy commandments . . . ? O
Jehovah, the God of Israel, thou art righteous; for we are left a
remnant that is escaped, as it is this day: behold, we are before thee
in our guiltiness; for none can stand before thee because of this.—
Ezra 9:6, 7, 10, 13-15.

See how plainly the concern with which this prayer is burdened is
the character of the people. Ezra's interest as he prays is moral; he
wants transformed life, cleansed personality, empowered manhood,
social righteousness. This week we have been noting some special
aspects of this central objective in prayer. We have seen how moral
courage, fortitude, power in temptation, spiritual poise and clear
vision of God's will, may all be won upon the inner battlefield of
prayer. Consider the vitality that such a use of prayer puts into the
religious life. It involves making God an actual partner in our moral
struggle; it fills our religion with practical significance. Gladstone,
in a letter to the Duchess of Sutherland, wrote: "There is one
proposition which the experience of life burns into my soul; it is
this, that a man should beware of letting his religion spoil his
morality. In a thousand ways, some great, some small, but all subtle,
we are daily tempted to that great sin." The sort of praying described in this chapter is the most efficient guard against that evil. It
makes the center of religion a fight for character.

*Strong Son of God, who was tried and tempted to the uttermost,
yet without sin; be near me now with Thy strength and give me the
victory over this evil desire that threatens to ruin me. I am weak,
O Lord, and full of doubts and fears. There are moments when I
am afraid of myself, when the world and the flesh and the devil
seem more powerful than the forces of good. But now I look to Thee
in whom dwelleth all the fulness of grace and might and redemption. Blessed Saviour! I take Thee afresh to be my Refuge, my
Covert, my Defence, my strong Tower from the enemy. Hear me
and bless me now and ever. Amen.*—Samuel McComb.

COMMENT FOR THE WEEK

I

If we define praying as "Communion with God," we naturally
think of it as fellowship with a friend, and so emphasize its peaceful

aspect. When Robert Burns bewailed the fact that he could not
"pour out his inmost soul without reserve to any human being without danger of one day repenting his confidence," he expressed a need
which is met in the lives of those who habitually commune with God.
Prayer means restfulness, quietude; men come from it saying,

"And I smiled to think God's greatness flowed around our incom-
        pleteness;
Round our restlessness, his rest."

As Jeremy Taylor described it, "Prayer is the peace of our spirit, the
stillness of our thought, the evenness of our recollection."

Now, praying is all of this, but none can think of it as dominant
desire without seeing that it is more. *Prayer is a battlefield.* When a
man, hungering and thirsting after righteousness, calls God into
alliance, he does so because he has a fight on his hands. He may have
set his heart in dominant desire on goodness, but that desire meets
enemies that must be beaten. "No man ever became a saint in his
sleep." From without, the influences of the world assail his best
ambitions; from within, the perverse inclinations of his own heart
make war on his right resolutions. A fight is on in every aspiring
life. Sometimes, like the captain of a ship in mid-sea with a tempest
raging and his own crew in rebellion, a man must at once steady his
course amid outward temptations, and hold a pistol at the head of
his mutinous desires. No one in earnest about goodness has ever
succeeded in describing the achievement of goodness except in terms
of a fight. "The flesh lusteth against the Spirit, and the Spirit against
the flesh," says Paul, "I buffet my body, and bring it into bondage."

In this moral battle, as in every other, *the decisive part of the
engagement is not public and ostentatious; it is in secret.* Long before the armies clash in the open field, there has been a conflict
in the general's office, where pro met con, and the determinations
were reached that controlled each movement of the outward war.
Even in law, "Cases are won in chambers." So, in the achievement
of character there is a hidden battlefield on which the decisive conflicts of the world are waged. Behind the Master's public ministry,
through which he moved with such amazing steadfastness, not to be
deflected by bribes, nor halted by fears, nor discouraged by weari-
ness, lay the battles in the desert where he fought out in prayer the
controlling principles of his life. Behind his patience in Pilate's

Court, and his fidelity on Calvary, lay the battle in Gethsemane, where the whole problem was fought through and the issue settled before the face of God. All public consequences go back to secret conflicts. Napoleon sat for hours in silent thought before he ordered the Russian Campaign. Washington, praying at Valley Forge, was settling questions on which the independence of his country hung. We are deceived by the garish stage-settings of big scenes in history. The really great scenes are seldom evident. *The decisive battles of the world are hidden, and all the outward conflicts are but the echo and reverberation of that more real and inward war.*

To be sure, prayer, which at its best is thus a fight for character, can be perverted to the hurt of character. Because certain temperaments are so constituted that they can experience a high degree of tranquil peace, and sometimes ecstatic delight, in protracted communion with God, the exaggerations of the mystic are always possible. "I made many mistakes," said Madame Guyon, "through allowing myself to be too much taken up by my interior joys." Nothing so hurts genuine piety as that spurious piety which is expressed, at its extreme limit, in the words of the Blessed Angela of Fulginio, "In that time and by God's will there died my mother, who was a great hindrance unto me in following the way of God: my husband died likewise, and in a short time there also died all my children. And because I had commenced to follow the aforesaid Way, and had prayed God that he would rid me of them, I had great consolation of their deaths, albeit I did also feel some grief." The worst enemies of prayer are those who thus speak much of it and revel much in it, but whose lives exhibit in ordinary relationships little of the trustworthiness, the "plain devotedness to duty," the thoughtful generosity and large-heartedness, which are the proper fruits of real communion with God. Jesus himself called his enraptured disciples away from the Mount of Transfiguration, where they wished to prolong their glowing experience, and led them down to save a demoniac groveling in the valley (Matt. 17:2-18). He would be the first to rebuke us for praying, "Lord, Lord," and not doing the things which he says (Matt. 7:21). The real pray-ers, however, have not thus weltered in futile emotion, supposed to be induced by God; they have been warriors who on the inner battlefield fought out the issues of righteousness with God as their ally.

II

As one seeks in the biographies of praying men to discover in terms of actual experience what prayer as a battlefield has meant to them, *he sees that for one thing it has been the place where they reconquered faith and reestablished confidence in God and in themselves.* Professor Royce, of Harvard, has given us this testimony from a friend: "When things are too much for me, and I am down on my luck, and everything is dark, I go alone by myself, and I bury my head in my hands, I think hard that God must know it all and will see how matters really are, and understand me; and in just that way alone, by understanding me, will help me. And so I try to get myself together, and that, for me, is prayer." St. Francis, of Assisi, used to sit in prayer by the hour, with no spoken word except the occasional exclamation, "God." Doubts, it may be, had assailed his faith; the clamor of the flesh had dulled the voice of the spirit; practical perplexities had distracted his life; and he went out from all of these to take a reassuring look at the Eternal. He "got himself together," and came back—"things seen" a little more obscure, "things unseen" vivid. Of how many powerful lives is this the secret!

> "As torrents in summer
>   Half-dried in their channels,
>   Suddenly rise, though the
>   Sky is still cloudless,
>   For rain has been falling
>   Far off at their fountains;
>
> "So hearts that are fainting
>   Grow full to o'erflowing,
>   And they that behold it
>   Marvel, and know not
>   That God at their fountains
>   Far off has been raining!"

This sort of inward self-conquest to some may seem impractical. They feel about it as a man may feel, who, not understanding what astronomy has done for life, goes into an observatory and sees the astronomer studying the stars. That the world needs ploughs and

looms and locomotives is as plain as a pike-staff; that the real
wants of men are on the earth, not in the heavens, appears so
obvious that this hard-headed man of common sense may wonder
what use could be made of a star-gazing tube that looks away from
earth and seeks the sky. But the fact is that the star-gazer sets the
clock by which we time our simplest tasks; he made the almanac by
which we measure all our days. We never caught a train, nor figured
time on contracts, nor set ourselves to any common duty, that we
did not put ourselves under obligation to the astronomer. Men never
understood this earth until they looked away from it. It never was
truly seen until it was seen in its infinite relationships. Galileo and
Kepler and Copernicus did not idly dream in impractical aloofness
from the needs of men: they rather fought out in their observatories
a conflict for the truth that has remade the world. So prayer is an
observatory. Even though our only solitude is that of the woman in
the tenement who said, "I throw my apron over my head when I
want solitude; it is all that I can get," prayer may still be our observatory; and there outlooks are attained that orient life aright,
that reveal perspective and give proportion, so that the solitary
conflict proves the redemption of every day's most common task.

III

The biographies of praying men show us also that *their struggles
for right desire were fought out on the battlefield of prayer.* We
said in the last chapter that prayer is real only when it voices an
elevated and purified demand on life, calling God into alliance. But
such praying requires in us the very thing we lack. Let a man try as
he will to set his heart on righteousness, the course of that desire
does not flow smoothly; it is impeded, sometimes halted, by land-
slides and cross-currents. The profoundest trouble in our characters
is our wayward appetites. The old picture of a Judgment Day gains
its terror not so much from thunder, lightning, shaken earth, and
falling mountains, nor from anything that these may signify. What
would cover us with unutterable shame is the fulfilment of the
repeated scriptural threat, *All secret desires known* (Eccl. 12:14;
Rom. 2:16; I Cor. 4:5). No one could endure that with equanimity.
When one contemplates the possibility, he becomes aware that the
deepest need in character is right desire.

Now, prayer has been the battlefield where the war against wrong desire has been fought out. George Adam Smith in a Dwight Hall talk at Yale suggested that no one had so frankly revealed this use of prayer as a battlefield for the conquest of desire as "Chinese" Gordon. A search of his letters to his sister reveals the truth of this. "I can say for my part," writes Gordon, "that backbiting and envy were my delight, and even now often lead me astray, but by dint of perseverance in prayer, God has given me the mastery to a *great degree;* I did not *wish to give it up,* so I besought him to give me *that wish;* he did so, and then I had the promise of his fulfilment." Even more vividly does Gordon put his use of prayer when he speaks of Agag—his figure for his own selfish ambition and pride: "My constant prayer is against Agag, who, of course, is here, and as insinuating as ever"; "I had a terrible struggle this morning with Agag"; "I had a terrible half-hour this morning, hewing Agag in pieces before the Lord."

Who can fail to see what Gordon meant? Some impurity was in him and he hauled it before the face of God and slew it there; some selfish ambition, counter to the will of God, he dragged up into the light and hewed in pieces before the Lord. Prayer is so often spoken of as the preparation for the fight of life that it is worth while to note how truly here prayer was the fight itself. Prayer, to Gordon, was no drill, where forms were observed that might add to the army's graces or even to its future efficiency; prayer was the actual battle between a wrong desire and a right one, with God called in as an ally. He went to prayer as to earnest business, saying with the Psalmist, "Lord, all my desire is before thee" (Psalm 38:9). Day by day he returned to cast down unholy passions and selfish aims and to confirm every true ambition in the sight of God. The very fountains of his life, the springs from which all action comes, were cleansed, until that injunction which Hartley Coleridge put into verse became the familiar prose of his daily living:

> "Whate'er is good to wish, ask that of heaven,
>   Though it be what thou canst not hope to see;
> Pray to be perfect though the material leaven
>   Forbid the spirit so on earth to be;
> But if for any wish thou dar'st not pray,
> Then pray to God to cast that wish away."

IV

The biographies of praying men show also that prayer was *the battlefield where they fought out the issue between the two conflicting motives that most master human life—the praise of the world, on the one side, and the approval of God on the other.* One distinguishing quality of superior souls is their capacity to discount the praise of men and to set their hearts singly upon pleasing God. We catch the note in Socrates before he drinks the hemlock, "We must obey not men, but God"; we hear it in Peter facing persecution, "We must obey God rather than men" (Acts 5:29). Such men were not so acutely aware of the public opinion of the earth as they were of the Public Opinion of the universe, in the sight of which they set themselves to stand clear and blameless. They lived as Milton sang of Abdiel:

> "This was all thy care—
> To stand approved in sight of God, though worlds
> Judged thee perverse."

At times the vividness with which such souls perceive the will of God for them, and the steadiness with which they do it, despite the condemnation of their fellows, lifts heroism to superhuman heights. Like the boy in school who pitched his best game of ball on the Saturday after his blind father died, because he said it was the first game that his father had ever watched him pitch, so these men live and work in the vivid consciousness of the "Father who seeth in secret." Their dominant motive is to satisfy him.

But such living as this costs a fight. God is not the only one whom we may try to please. Evil assumes its most seductive form when it appeals to this same motive—when some wrong-minded friend requests what good conscience cannot grant, or when popular taste sets the tone of living low and offers us praise if we will join the song. Sin in the abstract is hateful, but when it clothes itself in human flesh and waits to smile approval upon our compliance, it becomes tremendously attractive. Drink and impurity and all their ilk are horrible in theory, but dressed in the invitation of a friend, made alluringly incarnate in a person, what terrific fascination they may gain! Would Herod have slain John if the deed had not been pleasing to Herodias? Would Antipas have killed James and imprisoned Peter if he had not seen that "it pleased the Jews"? Would Charles IX have ordered the massacre of St. Bartholomew if his mother had not wanted it?

To be sure, there are times when to please God and to please some human friend are synonymous. From the time our only possible understanding of our duty was to deserve the approval of our parents, until now when the commendation of our worthy friends is life's highest earthly gratification, duty has assumed its most attractive form when it clothed itself in a person to be pleased. Stopford Brooke tells us that while gathering material for his life of Robertson of Brighton, he stepped into a Brighton bookstore and noticed a picture of Robertson upon the wall. "Yes," said the bookseller, "whenever I am tempted to do anything mean I look at that face, and it recalls me to my better self."

Many a living friend has so served us, and in the satisfaction of that friend's ideal for us we found duty no cold keeping of a law, but the warm pleasing of a person. Indeed, neither right nor wrong is often presented to our choice as an abstract proposition. They are almost always incarnate; they have faces and hands, and blood flows through them; they appeal to us with all the enticement that human flesh and a human voice can give. Because, therefore, to displease people causes us most acute unhappiness, and to win their approval is life's most poignant satisfaction, some of the severest battles in the moral life must be fought about this issue. If there is any commandment in Scripture most difficult of all to keep, it is this: "If thy brother, the son of thy mother, or thy son, or thy daughter, or the wife of thy bosom, or thy friend, that is as thine own soul, entice thee secretly, saying, Let us go and serve other gods, . . . thou shalt not consent unto him, nor hearken unto him" (Deut. 13:6, 8).

This conflict between the desire to please God and those who represent him, and to please the generation in which he lived was the central struggle of the Master's life, and he fought it out in prayer. We look at him now, across the centuries, and all his life seems singly set on pleasing God. To satisfy his Father was his motive, the possibility of doing it his joy, the consciousness of having done it his recompense. His great hours, such as his baptism and transfiguration, were blessed with the assurance that he was the beloved Son in whom God was well pleased; his idea of daily duty was

defined in his own words, "I do always the things that are pleasing
to him" (John 8:29); and when he thought of heaven and reward
he dreamed of no golden streets and gates of pearl—he saw only his
approving Father saying, "Well done, good and faithful servant."
But even with the Master this life involved an inward war. To please
God meant to displease his family, the leaders of his nation, the
venerable fathers of his people's faith; it meant desertion by his
friends and calumny from his enemies; it meant that he would be
thought crazy by his household, a traitor by his nation, and a heretic
by his church.

This great battle of the Master was waged in prayer, before ever
its results were seen in public. In many a secret conflict the engagement was fought out, until in Gethsemane he "offered up prayers
and supplications with strong crying and tears unto him that he was
able to save him from death" (Heb. 5:7). That sort of praying is a
real battle, not a dress parade. Jeremy Taylor may call prayer "the
peace of our spirits, the stillness of our thoughts"; but when David
Brainerd, colonial missionary to the Indians, comes out from one of
his Gethsemanes, saying, "My joints were loosed; the sweat ran down
my face and body as if it would dissolve," it is clear that Taylor's
definition is inadequate. *Prayer is a fight for the power to see and
the courage to do the will of God.* No man's life can altogether lack
that struggle, if he is to achieve dependable integrity that cannot be
bought or scared. The best guaranty of a character that is not for
sale is this battlefield of prayer, where day by day the issue is settled
that we shall live "not as pleasing men, but God who proveth our
hearts" (I Thess. 2:4).

v

To the great pray-ers the practice of prayer has meant this vital
struggle of which we have been speaking. On that secret battlefield
faith and confidence have been reconquered, right desires have been
confirmed, and men have gone from it to live "in the sight of God."
When men say that they have *no time for praying,* they can hardly
have seen the truth that prayer is this innermost, decisive business of
life. The time involved in the deliberate practice of prayer may indeed be brief or long. Whitefield, the great companion of the
Wesleys, used to lie all day prostrate in prayer, and Luther, in the
crisis of his life, said, "I am so busy now that if I did not spend two

or three hours each day in prayer I could not get through the day."
But Spurgeon, quite as good a Christian, when speaking of pro-
longed prayer said, "I could not do it even if my eternity depended
upon it. Besides, if I go to the bank with a check, what do I wait
loafing around the premises for when I have got my money!" The
length of time is not the decisive matter in prayer. "We may pray
most when we say least," as St. Augustine remarked; "and we may
pray least when we say most." With many of us time must be
divided, as is the land of the United States. The little District given
to Congress for the Federal Government, would on any quantitative
basis be most ill-proportioned. Texas is 4,430 times as large as the
District of Columbia, and even Rhode Island would contain it
twenty times and over. So one, regarding the brief time that a
Christian spends in deliberate prayer, might cry out against such ill
proportion, seeing how business and recreation of necessity pre-
occupy so many hours. But is not the answer clear? In quantity the
little District is small, but it is preeminently powerful. *The government is there.* Nothing goes on in all these states utterly out of the
control and influence of that District. Its mandates are over the
commerce and legislation of all the states; and every mooted question, not elsewhere resolvable, is taken before its Supreme Court
for ultimate decision.

Granted then, that our spiritual District of Columbia must be
smaller in area than our State of Texas, have we done with that
inward District what our fathers did in the nation? Have we
solemnly chosen it and set it sacredly aside? Have we located there
the central government, so that all power issues thence and all
questions come back to it for settlement? Is it apparent to those who
know us best that we would rather any other place in our lives
should be taken by the enemy than this Capital of our Country, the
place of prayer?

SUGGESTIONS FOR THOUGHT AND DISCUSSION

*What determines whether a man's good intentions will issue in
    action?*

Why do good intentions fail?
What are the enemies that oppose a man's dominant desires?
Upon what does their strength depend?

What happens to the man whose good intentions habitually fail to result in action?

What is the relative importance of time for preparation and execution in a successful achievement?

To what extent is a victory in a great public battle of life dependent upon previous victory in an unseen battle?

How far are right decisions in times of crisis dependent upon the controlling purpose of life? Where is this purpose determined?

What is the relation of secret prayer to public action?

What was the relation of the Master's habit of prayer to the controlling purpose of his life? What suggestions are given in the record of the temptations?

What place did Jesus give to time for prayer in the critical periods of his life?

What has been the relation of the prayers of praying men to their public action?

What great issues of life must be fought out in secret prayer?

Why does time for secret prayer give assurance of victory? What constitutes complete personal victory for a man in his life struggles? How far is it dependent on securing one's ends?

In these "prayers of preparation" what is the nature of the answer expected of God?

How far is it true that the longer the time spent in secret prayer the greater the victories in practical life?

CHAPTER X

Unselfishness in Prayer

DAILY READINGS

First Day, Tenth Week

And straightway he constrained the disciples to enter into the boat, and to go before him unto the other side, till he should send the multitudes away. And after he had sent the multitudes away, he went up into the mountain apart to pray: and when even was come, he was there alone.—Matt. 14:22, 23.

We are surely right in saying that the dominant motive of the Master's life was service. Yet we find him here sending away multitudes, some of whom he might never have another chance to address, and retiring into the solitude of the hills to pray. Was this selfish? Must we not suppose that he sent away the people, sought solitude, and gave himself to prayer, because he believed that by so doing he was rendering the largest service to others? Make real in your thought the truth of this; consider the increased power for usefulness that came to the Master in his prayer, the recovery from spiritual exhaustion and the fresh sense of God's companionship that he there secured. Are we not often shallow in our service and superficial in our influence, just because we do not escape the multitude long enough for the ministry of unselfish praying alone?

O Merciful Lord, who hast made of one Blood and redeemed by one Ransome all Nations of Men, let me never harden my heart against any that partake of the same Nature and Redemption with me, but grant me an Universal Charity towards all Men. Give me, O Thou Father of Compassions, such a tenderness and meltingness of Heart that I may be deeply affected with all the Miseries and Calamities outward or inward of my Brethren, and diligently keep them in Love: Grant that I may not only seek my own things, but also the things of others. O that this mind may be in us all, which was in the Lord Jesus, that we may love as Brethren, be Pitiful and Courteous, and endeavour heartily and vigorously to keep the Unity of the Spirit in the Bond of Peace, and the God of Grace, Mercy and Peace be with us all. Amen.—Thomas à Kempis (1379-1471).

Second Day, Tenth Week

And he said unto them, Which of you shall have a friend, and shall go unto him at midnight, and say to him, Friend, lend me three loaves; for a friend of mine is come to me from a journey, and I have nothing to set before him: and he from within shall answer and say, Trouble me not: the door is now shut, and my children with me in bed; I cannot rise and give thee? I say unto you, Though he will not rise and give him because he is his friend, yet because of his importunity he will arise and give him as many as he needeth. —Luke 11:5-8.

Notice the suggestive situation which the Master here describes. The one who prays is asking for bread, *not for his own sake, but for his friend's.* The need of another has made him feel the poverty of his own life; "I have nothing to set before him." How much such praying ought to be done!—by parents who feel their insufficiency in meeting their children's deepest needs, by friends who take seriously the fine possibilities of mutual service, by every teacher or minister or physician who deals intimately with human lives, by all in responsible positions in the social or political life of a community. Many of us, like the man in the parable, do not see how empty our cupboards are until a friend "comes to us from a journey," and then our barren uselessness, our ill-equipped spirits, our meager souls shame us. Such persistent importunity as this belongs rightfully to a man who is praying unselfishly—whose cry is motived by desire to have plenty to set before his friend.

Grant unto us, O Lord God, that we may love one another unfeignedly; for where love is, there art Thou; and he that loveth his brother is born of Thee, and dwelleth in Thee, and Thou in him.

*And where brethren do glorify Thee with one accord, there dost
Thou pour out Thy blessing upon them. Love us, therefore, O
Lord, and shed Thy love into our hearts, that we may love Thee,
and our brethren in Thee and for Thee, as all children to Thee,
through Jesus Christ our Lord. Amen.*—Anonymous (1578).

Third Day, Tenth Week

For as the body is one, and hath many members, and all the
members of the body, being many, are one body; so also is Christ.
For in one Spirit were we all baptized into one body, whether Jews
or Greeks, whether bond or free; and were all made to drink of one
Spirit. For the body is not one member, but many. If the foot shall
say, Because I am not the hand, I am not of the body; it is not
therefore not of the body. And if the ear shall say, Because I am not
the eye, I am not of the body; it is not therefore not of the body.
If the whole body were an eye, where were the hearing? If the whole
were hearing, where were the smelling? But now hath God set the
members each one of them in the body, even as it pleased him. And
if they were all one member, where were the body? But now they
are many members, but one body. And the eye cannot say to the
hand, I have no need of thee: or again the head to the feet, I have
no need of you. . . . And whether one member suffereth, all the
members suffer with it; or one member is honored, all the members
rejoice with it. Now ye are the body of Christ, and severally members thereof.—I Cor. 12:12-21, 26, 27.

Is not the truth which Paul here puts into his classic figure of
body and members, the basic of intercessory prayer? *"No man is the
whole of himself; his friends are the rest of him."* A man's bare
individuality is like the piece of grit that gets into an oyster shell, but
the pearl of his life is made by the relationships that are built up
around it. Let a man endeavor to abstract from his life all the meaning that has come from friends, family, and social relationships, and
he will soon see how very small his narrow self is, and how his true
and greater self is inconceivable without the social body of which he
is a member. "In such a kingdom," says Professor Jones of Haver-
ford—"an organic fellowship of interrelated persons—prayer is as
normal an activity as gravitation is in a world of matter. Personal
spirits experience spiritual gravitations, soul reaches after soul,

hearts draw toward each other. We are no longer in the net of blind fate, in the realm of impersonal force, we are in a love-system where the aspiration of one member heightens the entire group, and the need of one—even the least—draws upon the resources of the whole —even the Infinite. We are in actual Divine-human fellowship."

O God, Thou great Redeemer of mankind, our hearts are tender in the thought of Thee, for in all the afflictions of our race Thou hast been afflicted, and in the sufferings of Thy people it was Thy body that was crucified. Thou hast been wounded by our transgressions and bruised by our iniquities, and all our sins are laid at last on Thee. Amid the groaning of creation we behold Thy spirit in Travail till the sons of God shall be born in freedom and holiness.

We pray Thee, O Lord, for the graces of a pure and holy life, that we may no longer add to the dark weight of the world's sin that is laid upon Thee, but may share with Thee in Thy redemptive work. As we have thirsted with evil passions to the destruction of men, do Thou fill us now with hunger and thirst for justice that we may bear glad tidings to the poor and set at liberty all who are in the prison-house of want and sin. Lay Thy spirit upon us and inspire us with a passion of Christ-like love, that we may join our lives to the weak and oppressed and may strengthen their cause by bearing their sorrows. And if the evil that is threatened turns to smite us and if we must learn the dark malignity of sinful power, comfort us by the thought that thus we are bearing in our body the marks of Jesus, and that only those who share in His free sacrifice shall feel the plenitude of Thy life. Help us in patience to carry forward the eternal cross of Thy Christ, counting it joy if we, too, are sown as grains of wheat in the furrows of the world, for only by the agony of the righteous comes redemption.—Walter Rauschenbusch.

Fourth Day, Tenth Week

And in praying use not vain repetitions, as the Gentiles do: for they think that they shall be heard for their much speaking. Be not therefore like unto them: for your Father knoweth what things ye have need of, before ye ask him. After this manner therefore pray ye: Our Father who art in heaven, Hallowed be thy name. Thy kingdom come. Thy will be done, as in heaven, so on earth. Give us this day our daily bread. And forgive us our debts, as we also have forgiven our debtors. And bring us not into temptation, but deliver us from the evil one. For if ye forgive men their trespasses, your heavenly Father will also forgive you. But if ye forgive not men their trespasses, neither will your Father forgive your trespasses. —Matt. 6:7-15.

"When ye pray," said Jesus, "*say, Our*"—"*our* Father," "*our* daily bread," "*our* debts," "*our* debtors." Mark the fact that this prayer is not given simply for public use when many are praying together; it is directly related with the injunction to go into one's closet, shut the door, and pray in secret (Matt. 6:5, 6). Even when in solitude an individual is communing with God, he is to say not merely I and my, but our. The degree to which this social spirit in prayer will take possession of us depends on the vividness with which we perceive the intimate relationships that bind all men together, until each individual is seen not simply as a separate thread but as an inseparable element in the closely woven fabric of human life. "One man," said an old Latin proverb, "is no man at all!" To be sure, he is not. Rather every acquaintanceship is a live-wire connection between one life and another. Suppose that each one of us has a thousand acquaintances, and each one of those a thousand more, and so on over all the earth. Then we are completely intermeshed with one another. No two persons can be selected though one lived on Fifth Avenue, New York, and the other on the plains of Arabia, between whom, by many a circuitous route, live-wire connections might not conceivaby be traced by a mind sufficient for the task. Subtle influences run out from each and sooner or later come to all; no blessing and no disaster ever can be strictly private; common needs, common perils, and common possibilities bind all mankind together. "When ye pray, say, Our."

Once more a new day lies before us, our Father. As we go out among men to do our work, touching the hands and lives of our fellows, make us, we pray Thee, friends of all the world. Save us from blighting the fresh flower of any heart by the flare of sudden anger or secret hate. May we not bruise the rightful self-respect of any by contempt or malice. Help us to cheer the suffering by our sympathy, to freshen the drooping by our hopefulness, and to strengthen in all the wholesome sense of worth and the joy of life. Save us from the deadly poison of class-pride. Grant that we may look all men in the face with the eyes of a brother. If any one needs us, make us ready to yield our help ungrudgingly, unless higher duties claim us, and may we rejoice that we have it in us to be helpful to our fellow-men.—Walter Rauschenbusch.

Fifth Day, Tenth Week

Another parable set he before them, saying, The kingdom of heaven is like unto a grain of mustard seed, which a man took, and sowed in his field: which indeed is less than all seeds; but when it is grown, it is greater than the herbs, and becometh a tree, so that the birds of the heaven come and lodge in the branches thereof.— Matt. 13:31, 32.

The kingdom of heaven is like unto a treasure hidden in the field; which a man found, and hid; and in his joy he goeth and selleth all that he hath, and buyeth that field. Again, the kingdom of heaven is like unto a man that is a merchant seeking goodly pearls: and having found one pearl of great price, he went and sold all that he had, and bought it.—Matt. 13:44-46.

Read these words of the Master in the light of our thought about prayer as dominant desire. How plainly the petition, "Thy kingdom come" represented the controlling passion of Jesus! Prayer at its best always refuses the impossible task of separating the *I* from the *we,* and in its supplications gathers up the common needs of all mankind to carry them in earnest sympathy to God. It thanks God for communal blessings in which all share; it repents for communal sins in which every one of us who has thought selfishly or acted grossly has had some part; and it strives in earnest entreaty for social justice, international peace, the brotherhood of man, the triumph of Christ—every cause on which the welfare of all of us depends. As the Talmud puts it, "A prayer that makes not mention of the Kingdom is no prayer at all."

O Christ, Thou hast bidden us pray for the coming of Thy Father's kingdom, in which His righteous will shall be done on earth. We have treasured Thy words, but we have forgotten their meaning, and Thy great hope has grown dim in Thy Church. We bless Thee for the inspired souls of all ages who saw afar the shining city of God, and by faith left the profit of the present to follow their vision.

We rejoice that to-day the hope of these lonely hearts is becoming the clear faith of millions. Help us, O Lord, in the courage of faith to seize what has now come so near, that the glad day of God may dawn at last. As we have mastered Nature that we might gain wealth, help us now to master the social relations of mankind that we may gain justice and a world of brothers. For what shall it profit our nation if it gain numbers and riches, and lose the sense of the living God and the joy of human brotherhood?

Make us determined to live by truth and not by lies, to found our common life on the eternal foundations of righteousness and love, and no longer to prop the tottering house of wrong by legalized cruelty and force. Help us to make the welfare of all the supreme law of our land, that so our commonwealth may be built strong and secure on the love of all its citizens. Cast down the throne of Mammon who ever grinds the life of men, and set up Thy throne, O Christ, for Thou didst die that men might live. Show Thy erring children at last the way to the City of Love, and fulfil the longings of the prophets of humanity. Our Master, once more we make Thy faith our prayer: "Thy Kingdom Come! Thy will be done on earth!"—Walter Rauschenbusch.

Sixth Day, Tenth Week

Verily I say unto you, What things soever ye shall bind on earth shall be bound in heaven; and what things soever ye shall loose on earth shall be loosed in heaven. Again I say unto you, that if two of you shall agree on earth as touching anything that they shall ask, it shall be done for them of my Father who is in heaven.—Matt. 18:18, 19.

Jesus' words about praying *together* are quite as positive as his words about praying alone. We often quote this reference to "two or three," as though the contrast were between a few and a multitude; but in fact the contrast lies between social and solitary prayer. Christ means to stress the fact that he is especially present in a praying group. Praying *for* another, especially an unfriendly man, is a searching test of our relationship with him. But praying *with* another—how much more intimate and penetrating a test is that! If there is unforgiven grudge or impenitent unkindness or secret disloyalty, we cannot do it. As Jesus said, we must "agree." Prayer is a most effective cleanser of personal relationships when in the home, for example, people kneel amid the familiar scenes of daily life. The bitter word and the neglected kindness will quarrel with the mutual prayer; people must really be loyal to one another to pray well together. This is one of the fundamental reasons for public prayer, and in the family circle, the college group, or the church, the sincere and habitual practice of it will help any who genuinely catch its spirit to say Our—our blessings, our sins, our needs, and our Father.

Eternal, Holy, Almighty, whose name is Love; we are met in solemn company to seek Thy face, and in spirit and truth to worship Thy name. We come in deep humility, since Thou art so high and exalted, and because Thou beholdest the proud afar off. We come in tender penitence, for the contrite heart is Thy only dwelling. We come in the name and spirit of Jesus to make our wills one with Thine; to abandon our lonely and selfish walk for solemn communion with Thee, to put an end to sin by welcoming to our hearts Thy Holy Presence. Deeper than we have known, enter, Thou Maker of our souls; clearer than we have ever seen dawn Thy glory on our sight. Light the flame upon the altar, call forth the incense of prayer, waken the song of praise, and manifest Thyself to all. Amen.
—W. E. Orchard.

Seventh Day, Tenth Week

Simon, Simon, behold, Satan asked to have you, that he might sift you as wheat: I made supplication for thee, that thy faith fail not; and do thou, when once thou hast turned again, establish thy brethren. And he said unto him, Lord, with thee I am ready to go both to prison and to death. And he said, I tell thee, Peter, the cock shall not crow this day, until thou shalt thrice deny that thou knowest me.—Luke 22:31-34.

Ye have heard that it was said, Thou shalt love thy neighbor, and hate thine enemy: but I say unto you, Love your enemies, and pray for them that persecute you; that ye may be sons of your Father who is in heaven: for he maketh his sun to rise on the evil and the good, and sendeth rain on the just and the unjust.—Matt. 5:43-45.

Look through these two passages as through open windows into the habitual intercessions of the Master. We have been noting this week different forms which unselfish praying takes: praying for our own need that we may serve others better; pleading the common wants which belong to all of us; offering our entreaty for the coming Kingdom; and praying together in a social group. But in addition to these the Master prayed for individual people, both his enemies and his friends. His love was personal and concrete; when he prayed, he used names. Think of different tests by which we can measure the reality of love—such as willingness to render costly service or daily thoughtfulness in little matters. Consider then the quality and depth of love that are revealed by this further test—a care profound enough to express itself in sincere and habitual intercession. *When a man prays in secret for another, and does it genuinely, he must really care.* Put yourself in Peter's place and see what the revelation of the Master's love, expressed in secret intercession, must have meant to him. At the death of Robert McCheyne, the Scotch preacher, some one said, "Perhaps the heaviest blow to his brethren, his people, and the land, is the loss of his intercession."

Two or three days before Cromwell died, the Chronicler tells us, his heart was "carried out for God and his people—yea, indeed, for some who had added no little sorrow to him." This was his prayer:

Lord, though I am a miserable and wretched creature, I am in Covenant with Thee through grace. And I may, I will, come to Thee, for Thy People. Thou hast made me, though very unworthy, a mean instrument to do them some good, and Thee service; and many of them have set too high a value upon me, though others wish and would be glad of my death; Lord, however Thou dost dispose of me, continue and go on to do good for them. Give them consistency of judgment, one heart, and mutual love; and go on to deliver them, and with the work of reformation; and make the Name of Christ glorious in the world. Teach those who look too much on Thy instruments, to depend more upon Thyself. Pardon such as desire to trample upon the dust of a poor worm, for they are Thy People too. And pardon the folly of this short Prayer:—even for Jesus Christ's sake. And give us a good night, if it be Thy pleasure. Amen.—Oliver Cromwell (1599-1658).

COMMENT FOR THE WEEK

I

Of all forces in human life that go to the making of dominant desire, none is more powerful than love. Love in the family circle makes the mother's dominant desires center about the children, until no words can tell how cheap she holds her own life and how dear she holds theirs. In the nation such devotion makes patriots, consuming in them selfishness and fear, until they endure for their country's sake what they would never endure for their own. When one ranges through biography to see what desire has meant in men, he finds not only the sordid Ahab, the avaricious Judas, the licentious Herod, the ambitious Felix; he finds also men in whom devotion to people and to causes has made dominant desire utterly unselfish. A young lad named Müller, who was picked up from the river after the burning of the "General Slocum," bore this testimony: "My mother gave me a life preserver, that's how I got saved. I guess she didn't have none herself, 'cause they can't find her." Trace in this testimony the direction of that mother's dominant desire! So the controlling wants of the world's devotees, from mothers to martyrs, have been unselfish. Said Gordon in the Soudan, "I declare, if I could stop this slave traffic, I would willingly be shot this night." Cried John Knox, "God, give me Scotland, or I die!"

Indeed, what expression of dominant desire could be more natural than this prayer of Knox? The tendency to pray is shaked into action, not alone by crises of individual need, but by hours of masterful love. Men who do not pray for themselves will sometimes pray for others; fathers who do not think to ask God's grace on their own lives, find themselves exclaiming, "God bless my son!" If, as in Paul, vital trust in God is combined with devotion to a cause, the result is always urgent, intercessory prayer. "Unceasingly I make mention of you, always in my prayers" (Rom. 1:9); "Always in every supplication of mine on behalf of you all making my supplication with joy" (Phil. 1:4); "I . . . cease not to give thanks for you, making mention of you in my prayers" (Eph. I:15, 16)— these are windows through which we look into Paul's habitual intercession. He prays for the Jews—"My heart's desire and my supplication to God is for them, that they may be saved" (Rom. 10:1); for new converts—"To the end he may establish your hearts unblamable in holiness" (I Thess. 3:13); for the church—that they may "walk worthily of the Lord unto all pleasing, bearing fruit in every good work" (Col. 1:10). *When dominant desire becomes unselfish the result is truly represented in these prayers of Paul.*

II

In considering the meaning of this sort of praying we may well note, first, that *a man can pray unselfishly for himself.* Sir Edward Burne-Jones put significant truth into his saying, "There is only one religion: 'Make the most of your best for the sake of others' is the catholic faith, which except a man believe faithfully he cannot be saved." All that we have said about the service of prayer to individual character may be reaffirmed here as part of the unselfish aspect of prayer's ministry. When the Master said, "I sanctify myself," he was not selfish. A very unselfish motive was behind his care for his own life. *"For their sakes* I sanctify myself."

The vividness with which this motive in prayer will appeal to any man depends on his clear perception of the *intimate ways in which his friends' welfare and happiness depend on him.* Many a young man, rebuked for an evil in his life, has answered in effect, "My habits are my private affair." The reply which ought to be made to such a statement is obvious: a private affair is precisely what your habits are not. Your habits are the interest of everybody else. They are as truly a matter of social concern, if not of social control, as is the tariff, or the conflict between capital and labor. No man can keep the consequences of any evil to himself. They seep through his individual life, and run out into the community. When the Scripture says, "Be sure your sin will find you out," it does not mean "will be found out." It means what it says, "will find *you* out," track you down, spoil your character, destroy your happiness, ruin your influence; and because it does that, it will find your friends out, will tend to pull them down with you, will surely make goodness harder for them, and within your family circle will roll upon those who love you a burden of vicarious suffering. If a man *could* sin privately, he might allow himself the ignoble self-indulgence. But he cannot. Somebody else always is involved. The whole world is involved, for the man has deprived the world of a good life and given it a bad life instead. Sinning, even in its most private forms, is putting poison into the public reservoir, and sooner or later everybody is the worse for the pollution.

A man then has the choice between two prayers. Either he will pray for his friends' sake and his family's, for the sake of the girl he may marry and the children he may beget, for the sake of the commonwealth and the Kingdom which he may help or hinder, that he may defeat his temptations and live a godly, righteous, and useful life; or else some day he will be driven to a petition of the sort which Shakespeare put on the lips of the Duke of Clarence:

> "O God! if my deep prayers cannot appease thee
> But thou wilt be avenged on my misdeeds,
> Yet execute thy wrath in *me alone!*"

The latter is always a hopeless request. God cannot grant it. *No man ever yet bore all the consequences of his own sin.* The cross is a universal fact—symbol of the suffering brought on those who have not done the wrong by those who have. To pray for one's life in the light of this fact is to pray unselfishly.

Moreover, even when the fight with definite sin does not occupy the center of attention, a man for his friends' sake may well pray against the emptiness and uselessness of his life, and may well seek power to be worth as much as possible to others. Unselfishness is clearly the motive of such a cry for blessing as we have in the sixty-seventh Psalm: "God be merciful unto *us*, and bless *us*, and cause his face to shine upon *us*; that thy way may be known upon earth, thy salvation among *all nations*." Wherever real friendship and devotion come, prayer takes on this quality. When Quintin Hogg, with his Polytechnic Institute on his heart, during his last illness, wrote, "I would that I could be of some use to my boys, instead of the barren, dried up old scarecrow that I am!" he revealed the inevitable result of true friendliness. His desire to be at his best was motivated by his love for "his boys." Here we face the real trouble with our prayers. *Not for lack of a satisfying philosophy do our prayers run dry, but for lack of love.* We do not care enough about people and causes to pray for ourselves on their account. Let any one be possessed by a genuine devotion, and necessarily he will rise toward that union of love and prayer which Mrs. Browning put into rememberable words:

> "And when I sue
> God for myself he hears that name of thine
> And sees within my eyes, the tears of two."

III

Unselfishness in prayer, however, never has been and never can be fully satisfied with praying for ourselves for others' sakes. It involves specifically praying for others, and the more deep and constraining the love, the more natural is the definite entreaty for God's blessing upon our friends. The Master is our example here. The prayers of Jesus verbally reported in the Gospels, are not many in number and are few in words; but the indications of his habit of intercession are abundant and convincing. He prays for the *children*—"Then were there brought unto him little children, that he should lay his hands on them, and pray" (Matt. 19:13); for the *sick*—when a blind man is to be healed, we find the Master "looking up to heaven" (Mark 7:34); for his *disciples*—"Simon . . . I made supplication for thee, that thy faith fail not" (Luke 22:31, 32); for his *enemies*—"Father, forgive them; for they know not what they do" (Luke 23:34); for *laborers* in the harvest, since he must have practiced his own injunction—"Pray ye therefore the Lord of the harvest, that he send forth laborers into his harvest" (Luke 10:2); and for the *whole community* of his followers to the end of time—"For them also that shall believe on me through their word" (John 17:20). That the most unselfish life ever lived would be unselfish in prayer was to have been expected, and the evidence that he was so is clear.

When one, endeavoring to catch the Master's spirit, considers the various effects that may be expected from this kind of praying, he sees immediately that such intercession sincerely and habitually practiced, *will have notable result in the one who prays.* How much experience with vicarious prayer is summed up in that revealing verse with which the book of Job draws toward its close, "Jehovah turned the captivity of Job, when he prayed for his friends" (Job 42:10). Such prayer does liberate. It carries a man out of himself; it brings to mind the names and needs of many friends, making the heart ready for service and the imagination apt to perceive ways of helping those else forgotten and neglected; it purges a man's spirit of vindictive moods and awakens every gracious and fraternal impulse. As William Law put it, "Intercession is the best arbitrator of all differences, the best promoter of true friendship, the best cure and preservative against all unkind tempers, all angry and haughty passions."

For another thing intercession will often have effect in the lives of those on whose behalf the prayer is made, if only for this reason, *that the knowledge that his friends are praying for him is one of the finest and most empowering influences that can surround any man.* For Peter to know that the Master was interceding for him was in itself what a source of sustenance and strength! They say that Luther when he felt particularly strong would exclaim, "I feel as if I were being prayed for"; and in illustration of the same truth, John G. Paton, the missionary to the New Hebrides, writes in his autobiography, "I have heard that in long after years the worst woman in the village of Torthorwald, then leading an immoral life but since changed by the grace of God, was known to declare that the only thing that kept her from despair and from the hell of the suicide, was when in the dark winter nights she crept close up underneath my father's window, and heard him pleading in family worship that God would convert the sinner from the error of wicked ways and polish him as a jewel for the Redeemer's crown. . . . 'I felt,' said she, 'that I was a burden on that good man's heart, and I knew that God would not disappoint *him*. That thought kept me.' "

Many lives have been kept by knowledge of intercessions continually offered for them; and one need know only a little of Christian leaders, with their urgent requests for the support of their friends' prayers, to see what encouragement they always have found in the assurance that supplications were offered on their behalf. Melanchthon here is typical, rejoicing over his accidental discovery that children were praying for the Reformation. Paul writes, "Brethren, pray for us" (I Thess. 5:25); "Ye also helping together on our behalf by your supplication" (II Cor. 1:11); "I beseech you, brethren, . . . that ye strive together with me in your prayers to God for me" (Rom. 15:30). Cromwell writes to his admirals at sea: "You have, as I verily believe and am persuaded, a plentiful stock of prayers going for you daily, sent up by the soberest and most approved ministers and Christians in this nation; and, notwithstanding some discouragements, very much wrestling of faith for you; which is to us and I trust will be to you, a matter of great encouragement."

IV

In addition to these two effects, however, Christians have looked to intercession for a far more vital consequence. When *trust in God and love for men* co-exist in any life, prayer for others inevitably follows. Deepening intimacy with God, by itself, may find expression in quiet communion; enlarging love for men, alone, may utter itself in serviceable deeds; but these two cannot live *together* in the same life without sometimes combining in vicarious prayer. Now, such prayer always has been offered, not as a formal expression of well-wishing, but as a vital, creative contribution to God's good purposes for men. The genuine intercessors, who in costly praying have thrown their personal love alongside God's and have earnestly claimed blessings for their friends, have felt that they were not playing with a toy, but that they were somehow using the creative power of personality in opening ways for God to work his will. They have been convinced that their intercessions wrought consequences for their friends.

In this generation, however, with its searching doubts, its honest unwillingness to act without knowledge, its refusal even when faith would be a comfort to accept faith without good reason, this projectile power of intercession has to many become dubious. One reason for this doubt lies in the inadequate way in which intercession has been conceived and preached. To some people it seems to mean that one person may persuade a thoughtless or unwilling God to do something for another person. A popular analogy has tended to keep alive this misconception. God in many ways, so runs the analogy, refuses to work his will save as some man cooperates with him. The home life suffers, the government becomes corrupt, the non-Christian world goes unevangelized until men come to God's help. So intercessory prayer may be another way in which God waits for our assistance. If he will not do some things for my friend until I *work*, it may be that he will not do other things until I *pray*.

There is an element of truth in this analogy, but the limited application of the comparison is clear. God cannot save my family life without my cooperation, because he cannot take my place as son or husband or father; he *must* work through me. He cannot save the government without men, because he cannot take the voter's place; he *must* work through the citizens. And in the evangelizing of China, he cannot go as a missionary; he must find some man to go. There is nothing artificial about this necessity of human cooperation; it belongs to the nature of the case. But that God should deliberately withhold from a man in China something that he is free to give to him, and should continue to withhold it until it occurs to me to ask him to bestow it, looks like an arbitrary proceeding. It argues imperfect goodness in God. No true father would keep from one child a blessing that the child has a right to and that the father is free to give, simply because he waits for another child to ask for its bestowal. The trouble with such an idea of intercession is not simply intellectual; it is moral. That one individual, myself, should try to persuade another individual, God, to do for a third individual, my friend, something which the second individual, God, had not thought of, or was intending otherwise, or was arbitrarily withholding until I asked to have it given, plainly involves a thought of deity with pagan elements in it. And many people feeling this have given up intercession as unreasonable.

v

This surrender of reality, however, because it is explained in an inadequate form of thought, is never a solution of any problem. With or without adequate interpretations of vicarious prayer, earnest Christians in their intercessions are about a serious and reasonable business, whose sources lie deep in the needs of human life. A clear and rational belief in intercession must start with two truths: *first, the Christian Gospel about God; and second, the intimate relationships that make the world of persons an organic whole.*

As to the first, the Christian God desires the welfare of all men everywhere; his love is boundless in extent and individual in application; his purpose of good sweeps through creation, comprehending every child of his and laboring for a transformed society on earth and in the heavens. This, as Paul says, is "the eternal purpose which he purposed in Christ." Nothing that we ever dreamed of good for any man or for the race has touched the garment's hem of the good which he purposes and toward which he works. He is not an individual after the fashion of a pagan deity, who, like Baal, must be awakened from his sleep and besought to do good deeds for men. Rather every dim and flickering desire our hearts ever have known for mankind's good has been lighted at the central fire of his eternal passion for the salvation of his children. As Whittier sang it:

> "All that I feel of pity thou hast known
> Before I was; my best is all thy own.
> From thy great heart of goodness mine but drew
> Wishes and prayers; but thou, O Lord, wilt do,
> In thine own time, by ways I cannot see,
> All that I feel when I am nearest thee!"

Such is the Christian God.

When men go up to such a God in vicarious prayer, their inter-cession must mean casting themselves in with the eternal purpose of the Father for his children, "laying hold on God," not to call him to ministry, as though he needed that, but to be *carried along with* him in his desire for all men's good. Nothing is more wanted in the world than such intercession. The title of Dr. Mott's address "Inter-cessors—the Primary Need," is clearly the statement of a fact. God wants men to lay hold on him in inward prayer, aligning their domi-nant desires with his, until their intercession becomes the effective ally of his will. As in an irrigation system, with its many reticulated channels, the sluice-gate would not plead with the reservoir to re-member its forgotten power of doing good, but rather, feeling the urge of the ready water, would desire to be opened, that through it the waiting stream might find an entrance into all the fields and the will of the reservoir be done—so men should pray to God.

As to the second truth which underlies the reasonableness of inter-cession—*persons are not separate individuals merely, like grains of sand in a bag, but, as Paul says, are "members one of another."* The ganglia of a nervous system are hardly more intimately related and more interdependent than are people in this closely reticulated system of personal life. As Professor Everett once put it: "We ask the leaf, are you complete in yourself? and the leaf answers, No, my life is in the branches. We ask the branch, and the branch answers, No, my life is in the trunk. We ask the trunk, and it answers, No, my life is in the root. We ask the root, and it answers, No, my life is in the trunk and the branches and the leaves. Keep the branches stripped of leaves and I shall die. So it is with the great tree of being. Noth-ing is completely and merely individual." The more we know about personality, the less possible it is to draw clear circles about each of us, partitioning us off from one another. We all run into each other, like interflowing rivulets, with open channels, above ground and subterranean, connecting all of us. Even telepathy may prove to be true. So that if a man believes in God, in whom *all* live and move and have their being, there is no basis for denying the possibility that prayer may open ways of personal influence even at a distance. Personality, at its best, in its thinking and working is *creative,* and when in this love-system of persons, a soul throws in its dominant desire alongside God's, no one easily can set boundaries to that prayer's influence.

Indeed, there are certain aspects of intercessory praying where the consequences are plain. It is not a theory but a fact empirically demonstrable, that if in any community a large number of earnest Christians unite in unselfish praying for a revival of religious interest, that revival is sure to come. This can be tested anywhere at any time, if earnest men and women are there to do the praying. To say that this effect is simply psychological, is only another way of saying that God has so ordained psychological laws that vicarious praying by a group of earnest people does bring results. *So far from depreciating the value of intercession, this fact gives to it the stability of a universal law.* It names the conditions under which God does his most effective work through men. "For many years," says Dr. Mott, "it has been my practice in traveling among the nations to make a study of the sources of the spiritual movements which are doing most to vitalize and transform individuals and communities. At times it has been difficult to discover the hidden spring, but invariably where I have had the time and patience to do so, I have found it in an intercessory prayer-life of great reality."

While our minds are insufficient for the task of seeing to its end the explanation of intercession's power, our experience is clear that something creative is being done when in this unitary system of personal life human souls take on themselves God's burden for men, and in vicarious prayer throw themselves in with his sacrificial purpose. "Surely the man who joins himself with God," writes Professor Coe, "does not leave the universe just where it was before. All things are bound together into unity. I drop a pebble from my hand; it falls to earth, but the great earth rises to meet it. They seek a common center of gravity, determined by the mass of one as truly as by that of the other. You cannot change any one thing without changing something else also. The man who prays changes the center of gravity of the world of persons. Other persons will be different as well as himself, and he could not have produced this difference by any other means than this union of himself with God."

But no explanation, however reasonable, can do justice to the *experience* of vicarious praying. To feel that, we must turn to life. When a mother prays for her wayward son, no words can make clear the vivid reality of her supplications. Her love pours itself out in insistent demand that her boy must not be lost. She is sure of his value, with which no outward thing is worthy to be compared, and of his possibilities which no sin of his can ever make her doubt. She will not give him up. She follows him through his abandonment down to the gates of death; and if she loses him through death into the mystery beyond, she still prays on in secret, with intercessions which she may not dare to utter, that wherever in the moral universe he may be, God will reclaim him. As one considers such an experience of vicarious praying, he sees that it is not merely resignation to the will of God; it is urgent assertion of a great desire. She does not really think that she is persuading God to be good to her son, for the courage in her prayer is due to her certain faith that God also must wish that boy to be recovered from his sin. *She rather is taking on her heart the same burden that God has on his; is joining her demand with the divine desire. In this system of personal life which makes up the moral universe, she is taking her place alongside God in an urgent, creative outpouring of sacrificial love.*

Now, this mother does not know and cannot know just what she is accomplishing by her prayers. But we know that such mothers save their sons when all others fail. The mystery of prayer's projectile force is great, but the certainty of such prayer's influence, one way or another, in working redemption for needy lives, is greater still. It may be, as we have said, that God has so ordained the laws of human interrelationship that we can help one another not alone by our deeds but also directly by our *thoughts,* and that earnest prayer may be the exercise of this power in its highest terms. But whether that mother has ever argued out the theory or not, she still prays on. Her intercession is the utterance of her life; it is *love on its knees.*

VI

Let any man of prayerless life, or of a life in which prayer, an untrained tendency, is nothing more than an occasional cry of selfish need, consider himself in the light of this ideal of unselfish praying. To pray for himself for the sake of others, and to pray in vicarious entreaty for his friends, his enemies, and all mankind—this ministry he has denied. Let him not hide his real and inward lack of the intercessory *spirit* behind any confusion of mind about the *theory*. If a man honestly seeks the reason why a prayer like that of Moses is not easily conceivable upon his own lips, "Oh, this people have sinned a great sin. . . . Yet now, if thou wilt forgive their sin—and if not, blot me, I pray thee, out of thy book which thou hast written" (Ex. 32:31, 32), he sees that the difference between Moses and himself is mainly one of moral passion. We have no such high and commanding desires as Moses had; our wishes are lame and weak and petty compared with his; if every mental perplexity were overcome, we still should lack the spirit out of which such prayers spontaneously pour. Supposing that we knew exactly and held completely the Master's *theory* of prayer; is there any man for whom we *care enough* to pray as Jesus did for Peter? Is there any cause that could call from us his cry: "O Jerusalem, Jerusalem!"

The chief obstacles to intercession are moral. We live for what we can get; our dominant desires are selfish. The main current of us runs in the channel of our mean ambitions, and our thoughts of other people and of great causes are but occasional eddies on the surface of the stream. Even when we do succeed in praying for our friends, our country, or the Kingdom, we are often giving lip-service to conventionality; we are not expressing our urgent and continual demand on life. Our prayers are hypocrites. If the cause we pray for should suddenly take form and ask of us our share in the achievement of our own entreaty, we would dodge and run. All such intercession is clanging brass. "Our prayers must mean something to us," said Maltbie Babcock, "if they are to mean anything to God."

Before a man therefore blames his lack of intercession on intellectual perplexities, he well may ask whether, if all his questions were fully answered, he has the spirit that would pour itself out in vicarious praying. Is his heart really surcharged with pent devotion waiting to find vent in prayer as soon as the logic of intercession is made evident? Rather, it is highly probable that if his last interrogation point were laid low by a strong answer, he would intercede not one whit more than he does now. *Intercession is the result of generous devotion, not of logical analysis.* When such devotion comes into the life of any man who vitally believes in God, like a rising stream in a dry river bed it lifts the obstacles at whose removal he had tugged in vain, and floats them off. The unselfish prayer of dominant desire clears its own channel. We put our *lives* into other people and into great causes; and our prayers follow after, voicing our love, with theory or without it. We lay hold on God's alliance for the sake of the folk we care for and the aims we serve. We do it because love *makes* us, and we continue it because the validity of our praying is proved in our experience. St. Anthony spoke to the point, *"We pray as much as we desire, and we desire as much as we love."*

Of such intercession it is true,

> "More things are wrought by prayer
> Than this world dreams of. Wherefore, let thy voice
> Rise like a fountain for me night and day.
> For what are men better than sheep or goats
> That nourish a blind life within the brain,
> If, knowing God, they lift not hands of prayer
> Both for themselves and those who call them friend?
> For so the whole round earth is every way
> Bound by gold chains about the feet of God."

SUGGESTIONS FOR THOUGHT AND DISCUSSION

How far can a man say: "It is nobody else's concern, what I do"?

Is there a person so far away that no act of mine can touch him?

Is there anything which a person can ask for in prayer which concerns nobody but himself?

When can a person really pray the Lord's Prayer?

When is a prayer for personal needs an unselfish prayer?

What are the results of unselfish prayer?

What does prayer accomplish for the man who prays?

Why does the knowledge that others are praying for him help a man? How far is this a sufficient reason for unselfish prayer?

"Can prayer accomplish anything apart from the man who prays?" What kind of answers have we a right to expect?

Why is it necessary to intercede with a loving God for human needs?

What is really accomplished by intercessory prayer?

What place has reason and what place experiment in determining the results of prayer?

Why do men fail to practice intercession?